The CATTLE on a THOUSAND HILLS

The CATTLE on a THOUSAND HILLS

Knowing the Real God Who Cares about Our Real Lives

MARTY CAMPBELL

WESTBOW
PRESS®
A DIVISION OF THOMAS NELSON
& ZONDERVAN

Copyright © 2015 Marty Campbell.

All rights reserved. No part of this book may be used or reproduced by any means, graphic, electronic, or mechanical, including photocopying, recording, taping or by any information storage retrieval system without the written permission of the author except in the case of brief quotations embodied in critical articles and reviews.

Author Photo by Dan Hubbel

This book is a work of non-fiction. Unless otherwise noted, the author and the publisher make no explicit guarantees as to the accuracy of the information contained in this book and in some cases, names of people and places have been altered to protect their privacy.

Scriptures taken from the Holy Bible, New International Version®, NIV®. Copyright © 1973, 1978, 1984, 2011 by Biblica, Inc.™ Used by permission of Zondervan. All rights reserved worldwide. www.zondervan.com The "NIV" and "New International Version" are trademarks registered in the United States Patent and Trademark Office by Biblica, Inc.™

Scripture quotations from THE MESSAGE. Copyright © by Eugene H. Peterson 1993, 1994, 1995, 1996, 2000, 2001, 2002. Used by permission of Tyndale House Publishers, Inc.

WestBow Press books may be ordered through booksellers or by contacting:

WestBow Press
A Division of Thomas Nelson & Zondervan
1663 Liberty Drive
Bloomington, IN 47403
www.westbowpress.com
1 (866) 928-1240

Because of the dynamic nature of the Internet, any web addresses or links contained in this book may have changed since publication and may no longer be valid. The views expressed in this work are solely those of the author and do not necessarily reflect the views of the publisher, and the publisher hereby disclaims any responsibility for them.

Any people depicted in stock imagery provided by Thinkstock are models, and such images are being used for illustrative purposes only. Certain stock imagery © Thinkstock.

ISBN: 978-1-4908-8355-7 (sc)
ISBN: 978-1-4908-8356-4 (hc)
ISBN: 978-1-4908-8354-0 (e)

Library of Congress Control Number: 2015909151

Print information available on the last page.

WestBow Press rev. date: 08/26/2015

For Mandi,
who has walked through these stories holding my hand.

Contents

Introduction ix
Hoka Hey 1
Back to the Horse..4
Self-Doctoring..6
Afterbirth 8
Frank's Grandpa..10
The New-Fashioned Way..12
Simplicity 14
Jay, the Cow Goose 16
Tying Wild Cows...18
Cleaning Out the Freezer.. 20
Cody Bill..23
idroids...26
Old Feed Stores 29
Miserable Earl...32
The Guy with the Eye Patch...35
Healthy Work..37
A Story About Lilacs 39
Breaking Out to Win It 42
Great Challenges..45
Bull Testing...48
Diane and the Hot Wire..51

The Round Barn	53
The Two Pull Method	55
Warbex	57
Ranch Wives	60
JJ and the Kids	62
Even Keeled	65
Old Tack Rooms	68
Outsmarting the Wild Ones	71
Winter's Song	73
Cow Whisperers	75
The Top of the Ridge	77
Lonely Ticket Counters	79
The Good Fight	81
Paul's Miracles	84
Practice, Practice, Practice	87
The Mulberry Leaf	90
The Steens	92
Flattery Stinks	94
Grouse Flats	97

Introduction

I come from a long line of storytellers. I remember listening to my grandpa tell me stories about everything from World War II to pitching pea vines into a stationary viner to his brother-in-law crowing from the rafters of the dance hall in Troy, Oregon. My Uncle Merritt told stories about cowboys—some his brothers, others his heroes. And he was animated when he told those stories. My grandma said if you'd have cut his hands off, Uncle Merritt couldn't have talked. I agree.

The things I liked most about those stories were the lessons I was able to glean from them. For some reason, God gave me the ability to see life's reality, problems, and solutions illustrated in the form of a story. I suppose that's how I ended up becoming a storyteller, as well. As a high school agriculture teacher, I taught my lessons with stories. Vocabulary terms were defined through story, and soon enough, students would tell me that they would remember a certain term because of the "…story about you and your brother." Stories teach lessons, but more importantly, they show us truth.

Jesus taught a lot by telling stories. Some of those stories were true; some he made up on the spot. Regardless, they all held truth. And because of those stories, his listeners understood what he was trying to say. And it rang true in the deepest parts of their being. It's tough to get that from a lecture on do's and don'ts.

I follow Jesus' lead and tell a lot of stories to illustrate his truth. Those stories mainly revolve around the cowboy life—the life I know and love.

Because of that, cowboy-type people seem to relate, but more importantly, the truth seems to resonate with them because of the illustration. I love it.

When a rancher's wife tells me she has seen herself in one of my tales, or more importantly that she finally understands what the Bible passage at the end really means because the story connects the truth to her life, I feel like I know why God has allowed me to be from that long line of storytellers.

I hope the stories in this book open the reader's eyes to the life Jesus offers. He doesn't offer religion. As a matter of fact, he's not real high on religious people. He offers life—real life, life that never ends. All we have to do is turn from the broken heart of our gray and dead life, take up our cross, and follow him into that *real* life of freedom, hope, and love. That's an offer we can't refuse, and I hope that these forty stories will help draw the reader closer to truly seeing what that offer really is.

Marty Campbell

Hoka Hey

Anyone who has made the trek into Yellowstone in the wintertime has seen the magic of creation as it blankets the sage and pines of Roosevelt country in a ghostlike tapestry of moguled snow. The moguls are not placed there directly by the Creator, but by a nearby herd of bison who are shoveling back and forth with their noses, trying to find the grass underneath.

The sight is breathtaking, as is the sight of steam pouring forth from the giant Mammoth Hot Spring when it is not stifled by the shifting of the earth's crust. As far as my favorite spots on God's verdant globe, Yellowstone is amongst my top three. Whether my visit is taking place in June or in January, I see something absolutely breathtaking whenever I enter the park's boundaries.

As one travels from Yellowstone, out the Cody gate and toward Billings, he or she follows a road that leads through another of my favorite places. As summertime begins its descent, the green meadows straddling the Little Bighorn River whisper history to thousands of tourists who stand atop Last Stand Hill and gaze into the beautiful bottom where the legendary river oxbows through a litter of cottonwoods. From the arid, sage-strewn vantage points overlooking the Little Bighorn, one can step back in time to put himself into the shoes of those who were there on those two days back in 1876.

As the Lakota, Arapaho, and the Northern Cheyenne were waking late that morning, the furthest notion from their minds would have been an attack from the U.S. Cavalry's 7th Division. However, because of a lot of impatience on the part of Custer and a little bit of miscalculation on the part of the entire U.S. army division, those people were quietly invaded by an enemy who wanted to take their lives, whether that was figuratively, by placing them back on the reservations, or literally, through battle.

Although several war chiefs were ready to defend the encampment, they were not entirely expecting the attack. Nevertheless, they were not about to be taken prisoner again. Life without freedom was, in their opinion, not worth living. One war chief in particular, Crazy Horse, led his warriors into battle with a cry of *Hoka Hey*, which meant, "Today is a good day to die." Not the battle cry most of us would like to hear.

However, that's the battle cry that produces freedom. Those Indians believed in the freedom they were chasing enough to die for it. It was okay to risk life for that freedom, and as Custer's division found out, a man who is willing to die for something is a dangerous man, indeed. Custer's division was annihilated. Reno and his men were only a little more fortunate. Crazy Horse may have thought it was a good day to die, but his mindset is the reason he lived to fight again.

When we believe in something enough to die for it, it brings freedom. I read about missionaries who would travel to certain countries, and they would pack their belongings in a casket, knowing they would need one for themselves throughout the course of their mission. Yet they still went. Why? They believed in the freedom Jesus offers enough to risk their lives sharing it with others.

Think of what you would give up in order to grow closer to God. Would you quit your job, risk your reputation, sell your good rope horse? I've seen people get divorced over snoring or over football games. It's no wonder so many of us have a hard time hearing God or seeing him work in our lives. We're so busy looking at our own selfish, little stories, we're surely not going to risk them for some nebulous freedom that some dude who died two thousand years ago seems to be offering.

And that's why we know so many who are living lives of quiet desperation. That's why we continue to seek and build and store in order to try and fill those holes in our lives that things cannot fill. Only when we are willing to say, "Okay, God. I'm yours. My life is yours," will we begin to see real life. That's a fact.

Only when a group of colonists were willing to risk their lives and knock the chip off of King George's shoulder was it even a possibility to have a land of the free and home of the brave. Only when they said, "Okay. I'd rather die trying than live under this tyranny," did they become free. It's the same with us.

In Luke 9, Jesus says, "If anyone would come after me, he must deny himself and take up his cross daily and follow me. For whoever wants to save his life will lose it, but whoever loses his life for me will save it." It's kind of like that raccoon with his hand in the tree. He's hanging onto that junk so tightly, he doesn't realize he's trapped. Let's not hang onto our lives so as to lose them. *Hoka Hey.*

BACK TO THE HORSE

The first time I met Justin Bailey, I was working the ring at his father-in-law's bull sale. He began visiting with me like we were old friends, and I realized shortly into the conversation that he had been listening to a few of the songs I had written. The poor soul is apparently too easy to entertain. After learning more about Justin, I realized how great of a horseman he is, and there aren't too many people in the Northwest who will argue that fact.

His journey began as a rodeo cowboy—team roping, calf roping and riding broncs—but after school, he went to work for one of the West's great reining horse men in Dan Roeser. There, he refined his skills and his feel with a horse. I believe one of the greatest opportunities for Justin, however, is that he has since moved his training program to McKay Creek, out of Pendleton, Oregon, to the Anderson Land and Cattle Company headquarters. There, he is able to bring the best out of horses by working with them both in the arena and in the steep hills of McKay Creek, gathering the Simang cattle that pack the 7 Up brand.

One summer day, I was talking with Justin and his wife Shana, and Justin said some things that really impressed me. First, he said he won't take a horse unless he can have them for ninety days. Any less than that, and he just can't get them far enough along to give back to someone who isn't going to take the torch and keep putting those rides on them. More impressive yet is that he feels his program allows him to "get back to the horse." I like that.

To elaborate, he talked of guys we both knew who could get a horse to the point where you could win any rodeo on them in the team roping or calf roping, but those horses were not communicating with their partners. They were wearing all kinds of hardware that served as a shortcut, dictating to the horses to rate cattle, keep the slack out of a rope, or even run a reining pattern in a hackamore. But take them out of that arena, and they're lost.

Justin's philosophy revolves around communication, giving the horse something to do, and building a solid foundation that will allow that horse to handle any situation he might face, whether that's sorting cattle in a feedlot, roping in an arena, or holding a cow out in the pasture while his rider is on the ground doctoring her. Justin knows that once the big picture is taken care of, the little parts of the picture simply fall into place.

That same philosophy rings true in our walk with Jesus. If we have a strong foundation, based on communication, intimacy, and trust, and we move forward in the plan God has for our lives, we will become able to handle anything life throws our way without going gunnybag. That daily time in prayer, reading the Word, and listening for God's still, small voice is critical in our walk with Jesus. If we don't communicate with him, we can't know him. If we don't build a solid foundation of trust with Jesus, we won't be able to get through the wrecks without us trying to fight or flee.

Furthermore, when God trusts us with a task, it develops who we really are. If we never test our faith, how do we know it's real? How do we grow more faith, if we can't see that who we believe in will always come through.

The Bible tells us, in 2 Timothy 2:19, "Nevertheless, God's solid foundation stands firm, sealed with this inscription: 'The Lord knows those who are his,' and, 'Everyone who confesses the name of the Lord must turn away from wickedness.'" When a horse has a solid foundation on him, you can do just about anything with him, take him anywhere, perform any task, and he's not going to blow up with you. When our foundation is Jesus, he can do the same with us. He knows then that we are truly his.

Self-Doctoring

Self-medication is fairly common amongst cowboy types. Whereas the gentiles (as Baxter Black would refer to non-agrarians) are under the assumption that livestock medications are poisonous, cowboys are under the assumption that they are cheap. One must not haphazardly begin to give oneself shots of clostridium chauvei, though (although it inevitably happens at brandings every spring—accidentally, of course). As a matter of fact, my wife has ceased to let me self-medicate. She is in the medical profession and is soundly against the practice, as are most medical professionals, a group away from which cowboys do their best to stay.

Therefore, I offer this disclaimer: do not self-medicate, as it is frowned upon by medical professionals, and it could be deadly, too.

Nick Nelson, Jake Seavert and I were visiting at our weekly gather for Broken Horn Ranch Ministries about all of the ways in which we had cured our diseases with livestock medications. A friend that Nick and I had in common was having trouble ridding herself of a cold, and I jokingly recommended LA 200® or sulfa. Her aunt told her that her symptoms sounded like a sinus infection, and she had better see a doctor, because only antibiotics can cure a sinus infection. I told her that LA 200 *is* an antibiotic. She asked me the dosage.

I used to take a half of a Terramycin® bolus for my sinus infections, but Mandi has put the kibosh on that due to the fact that when they get stuck in your throat they really burn—and she got tired of shoving the balling gun into my mouth. Jake likes to take his Terramycin powder in his orange juice. Nick warned against the human use of Mycotil®, as it could kill you. None of us had injected anything into ourselves. We're not that tough.

Then Jake began regaling us with his successful use of Bio-Mos®, last winter. Bio Mos is a feed additive for calves that rids the body of bad bugs, increases feed intake, raises daily gain, and improves the immune system. He noted that his family was getting sick, while he was as healthy as a bull calf. However, he noted that he had put on considerable weight during the experiment, and soon, he figured he was performing as well as the calves to which he had been feeding it, gaining at the rate of 4 pounds per day!

Seriously, we shouldn't self-medicate unless we are properly trained, mainly due to the fact that it could be detrimental to our health. Doctors know what is going on, and many times, even though the drug might have the same name as its human counterpart, there could be serious differences in the makeup of the drug.

In our spiritual lives, we shouldn't self-medicate, either. Whether we'd like to admit it or not, many of us do just that. We go pray to God to help us; then we try to take the wheel from him. We try to do it our way, and we end up with a bolus stuck in our throat or some serious weight gain going on. We tell God we believe him and his Word, but then we walk out and try to do it on our own. Psalm 55:22 tells us, "Cast your cares on the Lord and he will sustain you; he will never let the righteous fall." 1 Peter 5:7 says, "Cast all our anxiety on him because he cares for you." True story, but how often does our life show we believe it?

If I go to my doctor and ask him to fix me and then go out and try to do it myself, I could have a wreck on my hands. When I ask God to work in my life, I lay my burdens down at his feet, then I pick them back up and run on ahead, I'm not exercising faith at all. Jesus is the great physician, let's let him do that work in us. We'll be better off in the long run. My wife will agree.

Afterbirth

When you live in the country with dogs, now and again something interesting shows up in the front yard. The typical question, "Where'd that come from?" is seldom answered in a solid fashion, but it's a sure bet that the dogs are always involved. Whether it's a deer hide, a cow leg, a China pheasant, or horse hoof, the dogs usually had something to do with its transport. Deetz, our old dog, was not content with dragging corpses into the front yard. She found it necessary to roll in whatever had died for what seemed to be a considerable length of time. She lived outdoors full time.

This time of year, we find a few more regular decorations out there than the sporadic artifacts drug in from out and about. As the calves start to drop, so do those wonderful other pieces of viscera that take the cute right out of calving. Generally, a cow will take care of the afterbirth herself, but if she's too slow on the draw, a dog will inevitably bring it to the house. In my days as an ag teacher, I appreciated this act from time to time, as I could take the placenta to school to dissect with my students. However, dogs will ruin a science project just as quick as anything.

Where folks in town would be quite grossed out by a little afterbirth in the front yard, we see it as part of the natural process during calving. A cow expels the water bag, it breaks, feet appear, the calf slides out with a little pushing, and the placenta separates from the uterine wall and is expelled within 24 hours. In the meantime, mama licks the baby clean, gets him to nursing, and in a couple of days, the little guy is bounding around like a toddler at preschool. Mama is usually doing well and milking like it's going out of style.

However, if a cow fails to expel that afterbirth, problems can occur. Truthfully, those problems can actually be deadly. Metritis can set in after a placenta is retained. If that's the case, the cow can get sick, she can die, or she'll be sent down the road because of the reproductive difficulties the retained placenta has caused. When new life begins, the old stuff needs to be gone, not hung onto.

That's a lot like life. We realize the gift Jesus has offered us in being restored and receiving the amazing life he offers. We become the new life. However, when that new life begins, Jesus expects us to turn from the sin that we'd been living in before. If we retain that sin, or that afterbirth, sickness will settle into our souls. It has to be expelled, so the new life can begin again. Hanging onto it will cause death. In reality, a dog rolling in dead viscera is a pretty good analogy to us hanging onto sin.

The thing about dogs is that they don't drag a whole lot of life home into the front yard. Everything they drag into the yard is death. The stuff they have a taste for is rotten and dead, similar to us in our days before Jesus. We would no more pick it up out of the yard and bring it into the house than fly to the moon, so why do we so often go grab the dead parts of our life and try to bring them back. Why do we keep going back to Egypt when real life is waiting for us in an intimate walk with Jesus?

The Bible says, "Forget the former things; do not dwell on the past. See, I am doing a new thing! Now it springs up; do you not perceive it? I am making a way in the desert and streams in the wasteland" (Isaiah 43:18-19). A new thing springs forth the same way a new calf does. That's why it's so important to let those former things go, to let that old way of life go and not keep going back to it. If we do, it will cause sickness, maybe even death. If we don't just get rid of it, it will end up in the front yard where the dogs roll in it and stink like the sin it smells like.

Frank's Grandpa

Frank's grandfather was in his prime around the time of the Great Depression. Folks around Benton County, Oregon didn't realize there was a depression going on; they were dirt poor to begin with. That didn't stop Grandpa from giving the best to his family. Through hard work, he was able to carve his living out of the land, running cows, cutting trees, and farming dirt. His kids had all they needed, and he had packed enough chivalry to buy the prettiest little diamond ring for his wife.

Of course, hard work was demanded from everyone in the family. Whether that was milking cows, chopping trees, driving tractor, or digging ditches, no one was spared–not even Mama. One day, while out in the yard doing some wood chopping, Mama swung a little too hard, and her most beautiful possession dismantled itself. The diamond in her ring, no bigger than the very tip of a knife blade, loosed itself and landed somewhere among the tall grass, bark chips and mud.

To anyone today, the fix would be simple. Go buy a new diamond. Not back then. Those were the days when an hour's worth of work paid one-twelfth of a day's wages; when a guy might have to hitch hike into Corvallis, because his family didn't own a car; the days when eating beef usually consisted of hanging and cutting it at home and storing it however you could without refrigeration–if you were fortunate enough to afford it.

Grandpa couldn't afford a new diamond, and that little stone was a very important part of the symbol of his lifelong devotion to and love for his little gal. He did some thinking, and in the meanwhile, he bought a bunch of chickens. He turned them out in that yard, and that's where he fed them.

After a few months, it came time to butcher the farm yard fowl. As Grandpa parted out each bird for eating, he sat the gizzards aside. Finally, after dissecting each, he found in one a sparkling diamond perfectly sized for Mama's golden band. Things had worked out according to plan.

I think that illustrates how patient and committed true love is, and patience and commitment are two qualities rare in today's world. If it doesn't come quick and easy, we don't want it. That's why the average credit card debt in our country is more than $15,000. We just can't wait and work, and if we can't have it easy, we don't want it. For many, that includes a strong relationship with God.

Proverbs 2 says, "My son, if you accept my words and store up my commands within you, turning your ear to wisdom and applying your heart to understanding, indeed—if you call out for insight and cry aloud for understanding, and if you look for it as for silver and search for it as for hidden treasure, then you will understand the fear of the Lord and find the knowledge of God." It takes the same commitment and patience to build a strong relationship with Jesus as it took for Frank's grandpa to get that diamond back. It ain't easy, but if it were, it wouldn't be worth much.

The New-Fashioned Way

Gary Marshall runs cows west of Burns, Oregon, and he's a mix of the old and new. He and his family are big proponents of holistic resource management, and they've changed their operation a lot over the years in order to make better use of their land and their cattle, and less use of their equipment and their fuel. They calve outside on the desert in late spring. They don't hay their meadows; instead, they run yearlings on them and cut them once into rake bunches "just in case". If they can go without firing up a tractor, they've succeeded for the year.

Some old timers are not believers, yet. Even though Gary and his son Colby, who used to work the ranch with him, look the part of the Eastern Oregon rancher—they do everything horseback, and buckarooing is an almost daily occurrence for them, in order to monitor the range and the cattle—they calve too late, and they don't put up hay! They spend a lot of time working with (gasp!) conservation and wildlife organizations, and they've created a pretty biodiverse piece of territory right on the edge of the Malheur Wildlife Refuge. It's actually pretty impressive.

Back when he and his wife Shelly were still on the ranch, Colby and I were out moving yearlings from one meadow paddock to another. They had the meadows separated with electric fence, and you didn't push those yearlings. You opened the gate, and here they came. The meadows looked mowed; they were so evenly grazed. And the wire grass had been becoming a thing of the past as the natural weed control continued to put pounds on all those calves. I asked Colby, "Did you guys mow this?" Nope. And he even showed me a whole bunch of bird's nests to prove it—bird's nests they used to cut through with the sickle bar of a swather. The practices were a bit hip, but they were also pretty groovy, if I do say so myself.

We, in the agriculture industry, especially ranching, often call ourselves true environmentalists. And really, for the most part, it's true. Who's out there moving cattle off of riparian zones? Who's out there managing noxious weeds through grazing management? Who's out there developing springs that are used by not only cattle, but by deer and elk, as well. Who's out there managing the biodiversity of the land on a daily basis?

Rhetorical questions aside, there are those who take it to another level. They don't just say they're doing those things. They don't just do them guess and by golly. They don't just do *those* things. They try *new* practices that look weird from a mile away and don't make much more sense up close. They go against what's accepted to do even better things. There are Christians who do the same.

I saw a quote from Stephen Colbert, one time, that said, "If this is going to be a Christian nation that doesn't help the poor, either we have to pretend that Jesus was just as selfish as we are, or we've got to acknowledge that He commanded us to love the poor and serve the needy without condition and then admit that we just don't want to do it." That's probably most of us. We stand on the party line that you've got to just pull yourself up by your bootstraps, and if you don't, then you're on your own. But that's not what God calls us to.

James tells us in chapter 2 and verse 14 of his book, "Dear friends, do you think you'll get anywhere in this if you learn all the right words but never do anything? Does merely talking about faith indicate that a person really has it?"(*The Message*). There's a kick in the gut for me! I'm like those by-the-book ranchers who claim to be the original environmentalist, but I don't have the blood, sweat, tears, or healthy pastures to prove it. I'd rather be like Gary and Colby, stretching, risking, doing crazy things for good. If we do that in our walks as Christians, think of the difference we'll make. If we don't, then Stephen Colbert hits the nail right on our head.

Simplicity

I first became acquainted with Curt Pate when he was putting on a colt starting clinic in Casper, Wyoming. My dad had known him for several years, so he and I had a lot to talk about when we met. I truly enjoyed visiting with him, and watching his colt starting demonstration was great. The thing I like about Curt is that he doesn't get too showy. It's not a circus act with him, maybe to a fault. I mean there are some of those clinicians who put on a pretty good show, and they develop quite a following because of it. Not Curt. He just starts a colt or works cattle and talks to the crowd while he's doing it. It's pure, and it's simple. No witch doctoring here.

As he put a start on that colt in Casper, I was impressed. He just did it like I've seen a million guys do it, but he seemed to really be paying attention to the horse. It wasn't like he was going from step A to step B to step C; he was moving with the horse. When the horse was ready to move, he moved. If the horse wasn't ready to move yet, or he just wasn't yielding the way Curt thought he should, he stayed right there until the horse was ready. There was no watch involved, but there also wasn't a real formula involved, just a simple rule to make the right things easy and the wrong things hard and get that horse to feeling which was which.

When he got done, Mandi and I were standing visiting with some friends, and we overheard a few old boys saying, "Well, that wasn't anything special. That's just the way my grandpa done it." No kidding. And that's really exactly what Curt was saying. He was just sticking to the basics of horsemanship. There was nothing magical about it. No whispering, except what he tried to say under his breath (which is hard to do when you're wearing a microphone). He simply put a nice little start on a nice little colt and did it as basic as a guy can. These guys were looking for some horse whisperer who was going to teach them to speak some mysterious horse language. I think they were hoping for some pyro to kick the show off as well as some sort of timed colt breaking event. They went to the wrong show. Curt's just pure cowboy, pure horseman, and I think he kind of likes it that way. He's there for the horse.

Lots of times, we try to find some magical formula that will bring us closer to God. We try to find The Secret, and we search high and low for that path that will make us better Christians. I've listened to c.d.'s on prayer where the speakers talk about mechanisms in prayer. I've prayed with people who use all kinds of flowery language. I've talked to people who just wanted to feel something more during a church service. I've known people who were appalled that a church had chairs instead of pews.

The thing is that Jesus doesn't want things that complicated. Sit on a pew, or sit on a rock; I don't care. What are you talking about? Mechanisms. He even tells us to bag the fancy language when we pray. When the teacher of the law quizzed him on the greatest commandment, Jesus didn't get all theological. He didn't dig into any dogma or doctrine. He simplified it. "Love the Lord your God with all your heart and with all your soul and with all your mind and with all your strength. The second is this: Love your neighbor as yourself. There is no commandment greater than these" (Mark 12:30-31). That's about as simple as it gets. What about the Ten Commandments? They're covered in these two. I like it. If we are doing something, as long as it is helping us love God with all we are, or it's helping us love our neighbor as we love ourselves, we're on the right track. One time, my doctor told me after I blew my knee out, "If it hurts, don't do it. If it doesn't hurt, you're probably okay." I like simplicity. So does Curt Pate. And so does Jesus.

Jay, the Cow Goose

The beautiful, spring mornings at our place hold a special place in my heart. We can look out our back window at Kanine Ridge, maybe see a wild horse or two, watch the ponies lying in the sun, and count the evergreens standing sentinel over the chaparral up on top. We are truly blessed to be able to watch the cattle graze through; although some years the grass doesn't grow as well as in others. We've got a couple of dogs that would gladly move them to some taller grass, but one spring morning, we had a new drover moving them around—a Canada goose.

It was quite a sight to watch that goose. Where he came from, I don't really know; and where the rest of his gaggle was is beyond me. It must have been beyond him, as well, because he was making himself useful by moving our herd of cows around the pasture. My dad came in, looked out the back window, and said, "I'll be hanged, there is a goose out there. I thought that was the chickens making an awfully funny noise." And it was funny how that goose honked and honked and tried to get those cattle to move.

Our puppy ran out there to chase him, and that goose took to the air and flew toward me pretty low. Then, he circled out above the horses, and finally landed right back where he had been. It was almost like someone had hollered, "Come by." I called the dog off, and that goose kept right after what he had been doing before being interrupted. He would just eat along behind those cattle, honk and flap his wings and look like he was trying to get them to move. I walked out there to check things out, thinking he'd take off when the dog and I got too close. Nope. He started to follow me. I was a little nervous, thinking he was going to jump up and bite me, like a goose often will, but he just followed me and honked a couple of times. Goofy.

Here was a Canada goose acting like a border collie, and trying his heart out, to boot. But those doggone cattle wouldn't move. They didn't even give the feathered cowhand the time of day. At least they'll hook a dog, but they just ignored that goose, nonchalantly feeding along. Although it built the goose's confidence a bit whenever they'd move, it was still pretty obvious that a goose is just not cut out to be a cow dog.

God has created each of us with a certain task to do—a specific design for our lives. And if we don't do that, the world must go without it. I don't know how many times I've told kids, "You can be whatever you want to be, if you just put your mind to it." There's definitely some truth to that. I mean, look at that goose. He put his mind to being a cow dog, and it kind of worked. But think of how much more effective that goose would be flying in formation like a real goose, adding his wing strength to that of the team and doing his part to get them to their destination.

God has given us each a *bent*, the path we were made to walk. When we see our children passionate about drawing, it doesn't pay to steer them toward being a veterinarian. They may end up being a veterinarian, but they'll never be as good a vet or as bright a light as if they had gone the way they should've gone. We are each designed for something that only we will be able to do. We each have a calling on our life, and the only way we can truly find out what that calling is is to go to our maker. Ephesians 1:11 says, "It's in Christ that we find out who we are and what we are living for" (*The Message*). Our gifts are there in order for us to make a big deal out of God. Can you imagine if Michelangelo had said, "I want to be a baseball player, not an artist"? Think of what the world would have missed out on!

We've all got our place in the world that God has carved out for us. If we seek him and seek where he wants us, our life will make a mark so deep, it will blow their minds. If we try to be something we're not created to be, we'll just be like a crazy goose trying to herd cattle.

TYING WILD COWS

Monty Miranda showed me how to tie a wild cow to a tree. Of course, we didn't have a wild cow handy, and our tree was a dwarf apple, but Super Bowl Sunday of 1995 became the day I learned how to tie a wild cow to a tree. I'd never had the opportunity to do such a thing, being from the wide open spaces of Eastern Oregon, but Monty is from Hawaii, and they have wild cattle, and they have trees that will hold them.

There were a lot of things that separated our Hawaiian friends from us. They talked funny. Their pidgin made them say things like "Tursdee", instead of Thursday. When they first came from the mainland, they wore hats that looked like they'd been thrown in the water trough. Some of these *paniolos* would actually bring their working saddles with them, and they were different, too. They had a lot more rawhide than leather on them, and the fork covers were braided down into the rigging. Plumb goofy looking. They didn't like the cold much, but the irony of that is that many of them ended up going to school in La Grande, where there's only two seasons-- winter and summer.

But there I found myself, in me and Corey Ashbeck's front yard, tying a bicycle to a dwarf apple tree while we dined on Rocky Mountain Oysters. It's funny I have no clue who even played in that Super Bowl, let alone won it, but I remember tying a bicycle to a tree with a chunk of rope, taught by a Hawaiian bull rider wearing flip flops in January.

It didn't seem to matter, however, how much difference there was between Hawaiians and us mainlanders. We traveled together, made fun of each other, and we've managed to keep in touch over all these years. Guys like Monty, his cousin Dusty, Vick Dubray, and Pete Andrade became friends, despite their funny hats and how hard it was for us to understand them. Man, we had fun.

God's behind that in a lot of instances. I think of some of my best friends. I couldn't stand a couple of them in the beginning, but in the end, God had torn down a wall and had built a friendship that lasts. I can pick up the phone, and the conversation starts right where it left off. Ephesians 2:14 says, "For he himself is our peace, who has made the two one and has destroyed the barrier, the dividing wall of hostility..." Jesus has come to break down walls between us, no matter who we are, as long as we are brothers and sisters in Him. All kinds of people live in God's kingdom. As I write this, I'm being preached to by a guy with rings in his lip as he sews a bag together to carry his little tracts that he gives away. Admittedly, he's not the kind of guy I'll hang out with on a daily basis, but I'll have forever to catch up with him. God has broken down the walls.

Cleaning Out the Freezer

I spend a lot of time in the livestock working facilities at Blue Mountain Community College. As a matter of fact, I took classes there, I've taught classes there, and now I preach sermons there every Monday evening. It's a pretty cool place, because generally if something has to do with livestock, primarily horses and cattle, it can probably be found in that particular wing of the building. Squeeze chute? Check. Semen tank? Check. Callicrate bander? You bet. They've got it all—which makes it an interesting sanctuary.

I took my animal science class up there a few times to peer into the working rumen of Nick Nelson's fistulated steer, Andy. If you really want to limit the enrollment of an elective class, do that on the first day. It eliminates anyone who isn't hard core pumped about the ruminant digestive system. Ain't nothing like the inside of a live animal to test your air.

One Monday night during our gather, though, I was sitting there looking across the room, and I saw a model of a yearling steer's ear. It was made out of rubber, and it did serve a purpose. Generally, an instructor can use a model to demonstrate where to place an ear tag or how to insert an implant. It kind of made me laugh to look at the rubber model. When I taught high school agriculture, I always preferred the real thing over the model.

Consequently, I became, over the years, a bovine body snatcher. I became good friends with many of the local butchers. They would call whenever they were going to butcher a cow, sheep, pig, or pigeon. I'd show up with garbage bags and a sharp pocketknife. I'd collect anything I could use in class and leave the rest for the rendering plant. Generally, I collected ears, reproductive tracts, digestive tracts, and various other viscera that could be put to use in an animal science class.

Unfortunately, none of that stuff lasts, so I'd put it all in my freezer at home. That began to wear on my wife. When she would go out and thaw, for dinner, what looked like some sort of meat, and it turned out to be a uterus, she would get quite upset with me. She finally kicked all those body parts out. Fortunately, it was about the time that someone had donated a freezer for my classroom. I took that baby to school, plugged her in, and began the transfer of giblets from my place to the ag room. That worked out pretty well. And I had lots of room.

People would call with stillborn calves, preborn calves, and anything else they thought I could use. In my vet medicine class, we had a major dissection project going for a long time. We'd just have to remember to thaw the calf out ahead of time. For most, it was disgusting. For my students and me, it was science!

Finally, things went south. Over a five day weekend, my freezer gave up the ghost. Unfortunately, I didn't realize it. Until the hall began to stink. My students and colleagues asked me, "Mr. Campbell, what's that smell?" I investigated, starting at the freezer. Sure enough, it was running, but it had become more of a refrigerator, and everything was thawed out. There was a puddle of blood on the floor below it, and it was beginning to get pretty ripe in that back room.

I offered two kids extra credit to haul the freezer's contents to the dumpster and wipe the structure down with as much cleaner as the custodians would let them steal from their closet. Those boys earned their ten points. Lesson learned? Don't store animal parts. Collect them on an as-needed basis, and employ rubber models from time to time.

We do that in life, though. We think, "Oh, it's okay to have this little bad habit, this little guilty pleasure, this little lie, etc.," and amazingly enough, we do okay for a while. Eventually, though, it begins to stink. We realize that inside, we don't have a collection of scientific specimens. We have a collection of rotting flesh that stinks and stinks worse every day. We cannot keep sin hidden for long. Eventually, its stench rises to the top and fills the classroom.

God doesn't just give us rules to see if we'll follow them. He gives them to us to keep us safe and out of harm's way. For instance, a guy could get away with a little lie. That leads to a bigger lie. Pretty quick he's lying a little money out of the till. Eventually, he's embezzling from the company. Soon, he's in jail. All because he got used to lying. The stench finally overwhelmed him.

We all need to clean out our freezers. Long after I had moved my collection out of ours, Mandi was digging through it. She pulled something out. "What's this?" she asked. It was one of my calf ears. It kind of grossed her out. That's a good reason to clean the freezer. God's Word says in Luke 6:43, "No good tree bears bad fruit, nor does a bad tree bear good fruit." If we have something rotting on the inside, it will never bear something beautiful. God wants us to get rid of the junk every day. If we don't, it won't take long to start stinking.

CODY BILL

Cody Bill Smith is one of those guys I've met several times, but he wouldn't know me from Adam. Regardless, he was always one of my heroes when I was riding bucking horses. I always thought both he and his brother Rick could handle their reins and get downright pretty on a bronc. When I worked and stayed with Shawn Davis in Twin Falls, I'd stay up watching his collection of old NFR videos, and I'd always camp out on those years when Bill was at the finals.

I've had the fortune of listening in on some of the conversations between Bill, Rick, Shawn, Harry Vold, Ned Londo and a few others from the golden era of rodeo as they told reride tales at the CNFR. The horses they rode were legendary. The lives they have lived are extraordinary.

Since Bill retired from riding bucking horses, however, he has stayed in the horse world with both feet and head all the way under water. Back in 1983, Bill and his two brothers started the WYO Quarter Horse Ranch Sale. When I first heard about the sale, I was extremely jealous. Here were a few bronc riders who got to spend all of their time finding good geldings, riding them for a year, then selling them for godawful amounts of money. One year, they sold a horse for more than $80,000. He wasn't some high powered cutting horse. He wasn't some supernatural head horse. The horse was merely a good, broke gelding that would be that way no matter how often or how seldom you saddled him.

I've run into a lot of people over the years who have purchased horses out of that sale, or at least purchased horses from people who bought them at the sale. None of them have complained. Bill, Jim, Rick, their nephews and brother-in-law always put good rides and lots of hours on them. They would rope on them, move cows on them, get them through rough country, and make outstanding horses. Many of us look at their model and dream of doing something like that for ourselves, but I will say that Bill Smith has a work ethic to beat anyone who would try. You can't turn out horses of that quality and as many as they sell without working year around and around the clock to get them that way.

There are a few good horse sales in the country. Many of them are production sales. Others are sales that draw consignors from all over. A few of us are getting ready to put one on, this weekend. We're selling just over thirty geldings, and they come from mostly different consignors. Bill Smith and his crew has done it themselves, and they sell a lot of horses. Now, it's just him, his nephew and his wife with a little help from his brothers. Bill travels the country finding horses, and his nephew keeps them ridden and turned into top notch mounts.

The coolest part of the whole story is that it should never have taken off. The logistics and odds of a sale like that working are next to nill. But, just as he never quit when it came to spurring rank bucking horses, Bill Smith hung in there until it did work. They've had high times and low times, but they've become one of the best sales in the nation. He says, "... it seems like it will come together if you hang in there."

To me, that is some of the greatest wisdom I've ever heard. It will come together if you just hang in there. That's hard to do, especially in our microwave society where everything needs to happen yesterday. However, most of us don't have to wait long at all for things to happen. What are those kinds of things worth, though? Good things are hard to come by, but when God pulls us in that direction, he'll come through—in *his* time!

I remember one time we were riding through some rapids in our life jackets. The Deschutes River was moving, and the rafting guide told us to breathe in at the bottom and breathe out at the top. I couldn't stay in time with the river, so I was sucking in water like crazy. I started to swim for shore, and it wasn't getting any closer. Finally, I just closed my eyes and paddled and paddled. Eventually, my hands hit the rocky shore. That's kind of what Bill Smith is saying. Hang in there, and eventually, you'll get there.

Galatians 6:9 says, "Let us not become weary in doing good, for at the proper time we will reap a harvest if we do not give up." If we don't give up, God will bring the harvest. Think of how many times people have given up when the victory was literally just moments away. That's not where God wants us to be. He wants us to hang in there, and it will come together for sure.

IDROIDS

I was talking to my friend Aaron Swenson about cell phones and idroids one day, and we remarked that there is nearly no way to escape their influence. I am being completely honest when I say that I cannot enter a room full of kids and not see at least half the heads pointed downward, staring at a piece of plastic. It's truly unbelievable how attached we have gotten to those things. He remarked that the only way to get away from them would be to go cowboy on a ranch somewhere. I laughed.

I responded that cowboys are some of the biggest offenders. A cowboy can be in the middle of Harney County somewhere, heading for who-knows-where at a long trot on the back of a pony and have his cell phone up to his ear. He might stop if he feels it buzz or hears it ring to check a Facebook update. The hardest part is undoing his chinks to get it out of his pocket. Many of my cowboy friends are more likely to text message than call.

Cowboys carry ipads, ipods, and iglasses with which to read their ithings. It's the perfect poetic tension, as a matter of fact. It all reminds me of a time an English professor of mine was critiquing one of my poems that hearkened to the romanticism of a coyote's howl 'neath a full moon. He said, "Oh, come on. Cowboys don't even live in that world, anymore. You're more likely to see them drinking a latte than coffee out of a tin cup." He was kind of right. Actually, he didn't know how right he really was. Cowboys and technology go hand in hand, anymore.

We've got eartags that are read with a digital scanner. We've got programs that will upload process verification information (what shots we've given to our critters). We've got electronic scales, email, Youtube horse training videos that we can watch on our smart phone while riding a colt. It used to be that to determine the gestational stage of a cow, or preg her, you had to insert your gloved arm into her…well…posterior and be able to tell how far along she was by the size of the grape you held in your fingers. Now, we've got ultrasound machines that can tell to the day when the calf was conceived. We can transfer embryos, we can keep our books on any number of programs, and our market reports are delivered via the net through the laptop in the pickup.

Somewhere, though, there's a cowboy who refuses to ride the wave. He may not be a letter writer, but he's sure enough not a Facebooker, either. To tweet, to him, is to whistle. Email is what they put in the post office box right next to slot F. An RFID tag is a weird way to number a calf. He just wants to swing rawhide and visit with real people and horses. Those guys getting fewer and fewer, though, and poetic tension gets even thicker. It's a strange dynamic seeing a guy on a horse with a phone up to his ear, but it's a tension that keeps the cowboy life with the times, I guess. I even used my cell phone horseback the other day. I'm a bit behind the times, though, because that was my first time doing that. I felt kind of icky.

The same way that tension exists between cowboys and technology, there's a tension that exists between loving and knowing Jesus and sharing our faith with the world in which we live. Maybe we don't like the new ways we have to communicate. Believe me, I would have quit Facebook a long time ago, had it not been for the fact that our ministry reaches thousands of people every week that we wouldn't reach using traditional methods. The world changes constantly, and, although we don't want to become worldly, we do need to realize that reaching the world with Jesus' love looks different than it did twenty, thirty, two-hundred years ago. Jesus doesn't mind that.

As a matter of fact, Jesus did things quite differently than the religious folks of his day. He sat out on hills and preached. He taught from boats. He walked around and told stories while people followed. He went into people's homes. He met people where they were, and he shared life with them. He still does it, as a matter of fact, and even though we may feel a little uncomfortable changing the way the Message is shared, we need to step out of the boat and meet people where they are the way our Lord does.

"Though I am free and belong to no man, I make myself a slave to everyone, to win as many as possible. To the Jews I became like a Jew, to win the Jews. To those under the law I became like one under the law (though I myself am not under the law), so as to win those under the law. To those not having the law I became like one not having the law (though I am not free from God's law but am under Christ's law), so as to win those not having the law. To the weak I became weak, to win the weak. I have become all things to all men so that by all possible means I might save some. I do all this for the sake of the gospel, that I may share in its blessings." 1 Corinthians 9:19-23

Old Feed Stores

I do love a good feed store. I'm talking about a feed store, not an *ag supply* store. I'm talking about the kind of feed store where there's a dock you back to, a wooden floor in the warehouse, and a few employees who know more about cows and horses than most of their customers. A feed store where the aroma of fifty pound sacks of combo, alfalfa pellets, rolled corn, and calf manna fill the air. That's a good feed store. I grew up in one of them.

When I say that, I mean it. My first job was working for the old feed store in Pendleton. Randy Johnston hired me for what I thought was a fortune to clean that old place. I thought it was the cat's meow. I'd had other jobs, but that was the first one for which I'd had to fill out paperwork. With a freshly minted work permit, I was ready to go. The crew was top notch, and they knew their stuff. As time went on, I graduated from cleaning the place to working in the warehouse and finally to running the counter. And I loved it.

The cool thing was that everyone there was pretty in tune to the agricultural industry, the cattle business in particular. Mike Schroeder grew up in ranch country around Unity, and he'd come to Pendleton to attend BMCC. His roots found their way to water, and he's still here, today, even though he's moved into livestock equipment sales. Nelly Hasenbank still lives on a ranch with her husband, Spanky. If someone wanted to know anything about lawn and garden items, she was all over that, as well.

Carla Rogers was the tack guru. She could rope better than most men and still does. As far as ordering tack, she knew quality, and she didn't mess around when she placed her orders. Carl Schulze, the Doctor, grew up on ranches all over the Great Basin. He'd gotten mail in Mitchell, Monument, Crane, and everywhere else they put sagebrush in the tea. Bill Taylor served the oufit on the tack and feed side until he let his agronomic urgings take over.

By the time I got to college, Luke Lowry had joined the crew. He and I had rodeoed together, and his family ranched the Owyhee Country around Jordan Valley. He brought with him David Jaca, another Jordan Valley boy who sat in the same animal science classes and ag construction and survey classes as I did at Harvard on the Hill.

It was the golden era, as far as I was concerned. I loved working there. When ranchers came in, we knew what they needed just by the time of year. If it was springtime, and Bob Lazinka backed to the dock, we'd just ask him how much salt he needed. He didn't have to say a word. Every one of us could run the seed mixer. We knew the products from dog food to parrot food to saddles to t-posts. We stacked hay, whether we were peons or managers.

In those days, the rule was to follow the order right to the customer's rig. If we happened to be running the counter and a customer came in and ordered two hundred t-posts and fifteen railroad ties, we'd fill out the ticket, place it in the basket or the till, hand him the pink copy, grab our gloves and head outside to load him. If you couldn't lift, you couldn't work there. If someone missed his ten-minute break as required by law, oh well.

In the summertime, the grocery store would call when their watermelon truck showed up, and one of us would head over with the forklift and unload them. They'd pay us with a couple of boxes of donuts. In the wintertime, it would get so darned cold, we'd have propane heaters going in the store to keep us from freezing to death. A few of the crew would commence to making branding irons, getting them cherry red on the heating element, and branding wallets and gloves and such.

If a customer ever arrived, though, they became first priority, and they didn't have to wait on a computer. We'd write the ticket, take the money and load it up. Customer service was top priority. I remember one time, we had closed her down for the night. I had set the alarm, locked the gates, and turned around and there was Raymond Doherty. "I need steel," he said. I unlocked everything, loaded him, and didn't change my time card.

I loved working in that feed store. Sometimes, I wish I could go back to those days, but that place is gone. That crew is dispersed. There's no going back. I still see all of those guys and gals once in a while, and they'll always be the ones who raised me, along with some help from a few family members. But that feed store is gone.

Once in a while, I'll come across a store that hits that nail on the head, but it's only a reminder, not the real thing. That's okay. Life goes on, and if we've always got our head turned backward, we never get anywhere. Luke 9:62 says, "No one who puts a hand to the plow and looks back is fit for service in the kingdom of God." Those days in that feed store shaped who I am, but if we ever try to stay in that place, we die. God wants us to move forward, taking what has built us up to what we are, and share his life with the whole world. But to do that, we've got to keep living it.

Miserable Earl

Wally Badgett has it figured out.

What makes Wally's cartoons so funny is that they're so real. His main character, Earl, lives the real life of a cowboy, and just about every real story you've ever heard ends up chanelling through Wally's pen into ol' Earl. From his mother-in-law's disdain toward him, to his poor luck in the ranching world, Earl is a guy with whom many folks can relate. He just happens to be the combination of everyone's bad luck wrapped up into one cowboy.

The other day, I was reading through a magazine, and I saw ol' Earl. He's a familiar friend, by now. As my eyes drew toward the cartoon and caption, I could see a lone cowboy straddling a horse out in the nasty weather. He happened to be riding along the side of the road, and a couple of passers-by had stopped their car, apparently to ask him a question.

The caption under the cartoon pegged it. The cowboy was being quoted as saying, "Yes, I'm a famous cowboy. Look in the dictionary under the word, *miserable*, and you'll see my picture."

It's funny because it's true. What other breed of person would subject themselves to the physical and emotional torture that a cowboy does? Surgeons undergo a lot of stress, but they usually don't come out of the O.R. with abrasions, lacerations, or broken limbs. Bankers put their jobs on the line for cowmen on a regular basis, but they're not freezing their keesters off trying to keep the calves alive. Firefighters are under a lot of physical and emotional stress, as are soldiers, police officers, and fighter pilots, but they are heroes when it's all said and done. Cowboys are just sore and cranky when they plop down in the chair at night.

I've come to the conclusion that it's a sickness. In every cowboy's brain, there is a genetic mutation that seeks out punishment. What other explanation could there be for someone who tries to outwit an animal who is 1100 pounds heavier and three IQ points brighter than he is? "Hey, I know. Every time we've done anything with that cow, she has either: a) run under my horse b) run over my carcass or c) blown enough snot in my pockets to lubricate a jet engine. Therefore, let's see if she'll let me tag that calf she just dropped."

Bummer! Wrong again.

Cowboys are similar to that fly who keeps trying to get through the window in the living room on a sunny day. They just continue backing up and running head first into the same wall hoping that it will eventually work.

But, we continue. Why? I don't really know.

I do know, however, that in life a lot of junk can head our way. And it doesn't seem like the greatest job in the world, but we continue. Why? Because it's our job. God, why do I have to learn this lesson? Because it will help you help someone else. I hate that answer.

I have a hard time, sometimes. I'm a preacher. I want to tell great stories about how God will *always* make life wonderful. But it isn't true. You can ask Paul when you get to Heaven. Peter, John, Matthew. Or just go to China or Indonesia or Iran or Egypt and ask those believers how perfect their lives are. But they keep going despite what the enemy brings against them. Why? Because they are sold out to the God who brings them a peace that surpasses all understanding.

So, when my day goes to the hogs, and I'm screaming at God, and I'm hating God with all of my heart, it's pretty tough to go and preach a sermon. But I will say this. God has *always* shown me the lesson just in time to teach it. And it's ugly. And it hurts. And more than anything, it's real. That's God. He's real, and he always wants us. Always. We may not get it all the time, but he's always there.

After Job had cried out to God, questioned him, doubted him, God put him in his place. He humbled Job with a good line of questioning, making Job realize how little of a grasp he truly had on the situation. Been there. Done that. Finally, Job responded, "I know that you can do all things; no purpose of yours can be thwarted. You asked, 'Who is this that obscures my plans without knowledge?' Surely I spoke of things I did not understand, things too wonderful for me to know. You said, 'Listen now, and I will speak; I will question you, and you shall answer me.' My ears had heard of you but now my eyes have seen you. Therefore I despise myself and repent in dust and ashes." (Job 42:2-6)

The Guy with the Eye Patch

For a long time, Bill Owen was referred to by my son as "the guy with the eye patch". Soon, however, he became known by "the guy whose paintings look like photos." Crae and I would often study the Arizona artist's paintings with an intensity five year olds generally reserve for catching frogs. Crae would pore over the detail, and he would go and try to emulate Bill Owen in his own drawings and paintings.

I think the thing I admired most about Bill Owen was that he wasn't just a cowboy artist; he was a cowboy. Having been born to a ranching family, he grew up popping brush in Arizona and built a frame of reference unparalleled by nearly anyone since Charlie Russell. When he did his research, he applied his familiarity with the equipment, the country, the plans, and even the *ruined* plans of the Arizona cowboy. He was for real, and it shows in his work.

However much he was a cowboy, though, Bill Owen was an artist. He used to work eight hours a day, seven days a week, on art. He pared that back to six days a week, later in life, but according to his wife, Valerie, it wasn't a "*have* to." Painting and sculpting were like breathing to Bill Owen. She said for Bill, he wasn't able to *not* create artwork. It's who he was, more than even being a cowboy. Having purchased a ranch several years back, Bill had accomplished a lifelong dream, but the ranching was taking away from his artwork, so he sold out and went back to his passion.

If one looks at Bill Owen's paintings, the enthusiasm for his subject matter is so evident. That's what makes them so real and so right. The dust coming off of a horse's foot, the sun glowing on the rocks surrounding a kid bringing in a wild cow, the bulldog taps on a cowboy's stirrups, the ragged denim shirts and batwing chaps. He wasn't just painting; he was putting himself into his art the way a parent does his children.

As far as I'm concerned, the "guy with the eye patch" is truly an example of what happens when we grasp what God has planned for us. When we listen to that still, small voice that says, "You were made for this," and we pull up stakes and follow it, we come to life, and our light, our life, shines before men. Too many times, that voice is drowned out by logic, by lesser dreams, by society, by greed. That song, "Flashdance," tells us to take our passion and make it happen. However, I don't think it hits the nail quite square. When we find our passion, if we let go of the reins and pour ourselves into it, it will have no choice but to happen.

Psalm 139:13-15 cries out to God. "For you created my inmost being; you knit me together in my mother's womb. I praise you because I am fearfully and wonderfully made; your works are wonderful, I know that full well. My frame was not hidden from you when I was made in the secret place, when I was woven together in the depths of the earth." God has created each of us with a *frame* that is *fearfully and wonderfully made*. For some, that's painting pictures. For others, it's speaking to crowds of people. Some come alive when they begin to crunch numbers together. Regardless, we all need to fall into God's plan for our lives. It's never too late, and we've all seen what happens to people who do.

Healthy Work

Working for the Stone Hereford Ranch was one of the healthiest things my grandpa, Bob Campbell, ever did. For most cowboys, his was a dream job. He didn't build fence, drive tractors, or even drive a feed truck very much. His job consisted of riding good horses through herds of Hereford cattle, checking health, roping the sick ones, and doctoring them in the pasture next to Mama. He truly made his living with his rope.

Even though riding under the blue skies of Eastern Oregon filled his lungs with clean air and kept a smile on his face for most of each day, that wasn't the healthy part of the job. When he first started the job, he'd ride around the ranch and the lots with a cigarette hanging from his lips most of the day. Fresh air has a hard time getting through those filters.

The job carried a lot of good things with it, but they weren't the healthiest parts. He got to take his teenage kids on as hands once in a while, but that wasn't always the healthiest thing in the world. He got to meet great cattlemen from all over the West as they came to purchase seedstock for their operations. He even got offered a job working for John Wayne on his Arizona spread at one time, but even that buoy to his confidence wasn't the healthiest part of his job.

The healthy part of his job was the exercise that came with it. Riding isn't a whole lot of work, of course, unless you're posting a trot around a twenty-five thousand acre circle, and there weren't any of those on the Stone spread. Roping will exercise your arm a little, but not to the extent recommended by most P.E. teachers. He had things set up so he didn't have to get off to open gates, so that rules that out, as well.

No, the exercise came when he had to doctor a calf. Roping one and getting the calf veterinary care without help proved to be a challenge, sometimes. He had a number of ways of getting it done, and with bigger cattle, it seemed to be a little easier. He could lay trips, tangle legs, and perform a number of tasks that were set up to get cattle on the ground. However, little guys always threw him a curve, probably because they seemed like they'd be so easy.

One time, he was riding through a bunch and saw a droopy headed baby calf who seemed to have a combiotic deficiency of some sort. It just so happened that Howard Stone and a couple of buyers happened to be out there looking at that bunch of cattle at the same time. Not one to get too nervous in front of an audience, Grandpa rode in and quietly roped the calf by a neck and front leg. He was tied off hard and fast, so he got off and moved in to get him on the ground.

Unfortunately, the little booger was healthier than he appeared. For a good long minute, Grandpa wrestled that calf while his horse worked the rope. Unfortunately, all those cigarettes had diminished his lung capacity, and he had gotten winded to the point of almost having to lose his breakfast. All this took place in front of an audience, and when he finally got the calf flanked and on the ground, he looked up to see them watching him gasp for air. The heaves came hard and fast, and between them, he looked up at the gentlemen watching, looked in his shirt pocket at his pack of smokes, reached in and threw the pack on the ground. He never smoked another cigarette again.

Sometimes, healthy comes after a struggle. We make the right choice only after we see how bad the wrong choice has treated us. God will allow us to make the wrong choice, but sometimes, he'll throw a challenge at us we can't handle because of the life we're living. I'm thankful for those lessons. They help us move ahead in life and leave those things that are killing us behind. Proverbs 22:3 says, "The prudent see danger and take refuge, but the simple keep going and pay the penalty." If we see something is hurting us, and we don't throw it away, we're pretty simple, indeed.

A Story About Lilacs

This is a story about lilacs. Kind of.

Back in 2000, I announced two rodeos for Glen Herriman of the Northern Cross Rodeo Company. I was filling in for Steve Kenyon at both of them, so I took Steve's sound system with me to Deer Park, the first of the two. I had no clue how to set it up, and Glen looked pretty concerned. Mandi even heard him mumble, "What kind of an announcer doesn't know how to run a sound system?" I still don't know how. Needless to say, he was wondering what exactly Steve had sent to him.

At the end of that performance, Glen came up to me and shook my hand. He was excited about what he had gotten himself into, and that continued over the next three performances I announced for him.

That winter, Glen called me and asked me if I'd be interested in announcing all of his rodeos. He was offering me fifteen of them, and he was going to join the PRCA that year. He'd just take me with him. I told him I'd think about it, and after a day or two of thought, I turned him down. I didn't want to be an announcer. I was a bronc rider: kind of like Happy Gilmore was a hockey player.

In 2010, Mandi and I decided I'd better go after the announcing deal eleven years after turning down a pretty big break. I hung my shingle out and got one rodeo the first year. The next year, I had eight. The following year, I doubled that and got my PRCA card. However, that doesn't keep me from kicking myself for not jumping on that chance fourteen years ago.

I often think of where I'd be right now if I had; and there have been times I wonder what God thought of me turning that down.

That brings me to the lilacs. Lilacs are my favorite flower. Probably the reason I like them so much is that they're here for so little time. When I was growing up, we had a lilac bush outside our kitchen window, and in the spring, when they were blooming, I would sit there and eat my cereal to the aroma of a beautiful purple flower that was to go away very soon. Now, as an adult, I have a lilac bush right outside my front door, and I breathe them in for all I am worth, because they fade into the summer in a couple of weeks' time.

In June of 2013, I was driving in the country around Jackson Hole, Wyoming. I was on my way to the College National Finals Rodeo in Casper, and as I drove through a little town in the hills on the Idaho/Wyoming border, I began to smell lilacs. Our lilacs had been gone for weeks, yet that town had blooming lilacs everywhere! I thought I was in Heaven! As I was enjoying the aroma of those beautiful flowers, I could hear God speaking to my heart in a big way. He was saying, "Look, here. I'm giving you another chance to smell the lilacs. I'm giving you another chance."

I smiled and realized how awesome our God really is. You see, I was on my way to the CNFR to announce the first two performances of one of the greatest rodeos in the world alongside Boyd Polhamus, a guy who has announced more NFRs than anyone in the world, other than Bob Tallman. I had turned down that opportunity once, but God had opened the doors again.

Those first two performances were great. I was standing beside a guy I've studied for years, and we truly shared the stage along with Justin Rumford, the PRCA's Clown of the Year. What a blast! When it was all said and done, and when my visits with Boyd were through, I felt like I had done what God had allowed me a second chance at, and I had done it well. That's a God thing. I just do the talking.

In 2 Kings 8, a widow whose son Elisha has brought back from the dead, leaves her home for seven years because of a famine. When she returns, she finds a squatter who has been living in her home and farming her ground. She tells him it's her place, and he tells her to take a hike. She goes to the king, who has just heard the story about Elisha healing her son, and nearly at that moment, she pleads her case. The king finds out she's the widow from the amazing tale, and he takes care of her. "The king asked the woman about it, and she told him. Then he assigned an official to her case and said to him, 'Give back everything that belonged to her, including all the income from her land from the day she left the country until now.'" She got it all back.

I thought once the lilacs faded, I'd not get to smell them again, not until next year. God said otherwise. He said, "Here's another chance to smell the lilacs." I plucked a couple of lilacs off of the bush at my hotel in Jackson and kept them in my car all the way to Casper. God will restore everything he wanted us to have in the first place if we just follow him. I'm so thankful I got to smell the lilacs again.

Breaking Out to Win It

I broke out to win it.

That's the most backward saying I've ever heard. But I've heard it a million times. "How'd you do this weekend?" I'll ask a timed event cowboy.

"Well, I broke out to win it."

"You broke out, and you still won?" I'll ask sarcastically.

Then the fight is on. The timey tries to explain that he would have won it had he not broke out. If he had given the calf or steer the allotted head start out of the roping chute, he would have won the rodeo. Hmmm, I say. Then I walk away.

However, I have the pen, and now I'll express my true feelings on the subject. Nobody breaks out to win it. Of course, a lot of it depends on how bad a person breaks the barrier, but regardless, if he broke the barrier, it's because he left the box a tick too soon. Maybe three or four ticks. But there's the rub. That doesn't just mean that they'd add a tenth of a second to the time and call it good. It starts a complete change of events.

If a roper leaves a tenth too soon, he breaks the barrier, and he ropes his calf two strides from the box, and the run goes smoothly, he could be 7.5 seconds—plus ten. The winning time was 7.6, no penalty. Cowboy logic says, "I broke out, or I'd have won it." Really, though, if he had left a tenth of a second later, that could possibly add a stride of separation between his horse and the calf. That stride does a few things. One, it changes the angle of the loop needed to catch the calf. Two, it causes the cowboy to have to swing another swing in order to get into position to throw the loop he would have thrown in his breakout run.

Perhaps he decides to reach. Then the odds enter in. Perhaps the calf has a mallard in him on that third stride, and the cowboy has to adjust his horse's direction to get to where the calf is in his sights. That adds time. Maybe in that one stride, the calf stumbles. Maybe to reach, the cowboy feeds a hair more slack which then comes around and figure eights around the calf's tail, adding who-knows-how-many seconds to the run. Anything can happen.

One time, I ran into a pickup that turned without a blinker while I was passing it. Had I dropped my keys when I got into my pickup, that would have put me a couple of seconds further behind the pickup at that turn. Had I decided to put a different tape in or set my cruise at 65 instead of 67, I would have missed him altogether, and I'd still have that pickup and better insurance rates. Had I ridden better and not fallen off so many horses, I'd have been a world champion saddle bronc rider. Nobody breaks out to win it.

Too many times, we do the same thing in our lives. We go to a place my old pastor calls "The Land of Woulda Shoulda Coulda." If this, if that, and then we fight our heads over everything. Sometimes we win, and sometimes we lose, but through it all, God works for the good.

I heard an interview with Steven Curtis Chapman right after he had lost his daughter to a tragic accident. She was only five, and her big brother was backing a car out of the driveway when he ran over her. Steven Curtis said he knew the Bible said all of our days are ordained and numbered by God, and that gave him peace. There were fewer *what-ifs* about her life. She had lived her life completely, and he said, "I didn't feel like we'd been robbed of all those years she might have lived. She wasn't meant to live those years."

When we start to play the *what-might-have-been* game, we are showing a lack of faith in God's story. We all do it. However, more and more I see that God has an amazing way of making everything come together. Regrets are a waste of time. We need only keep going forward. Isaiah 58:11 says, "The Lord will guide you always; he will satisfy your needs in a sun-scorched land and will strengthen your frame. You will be like a well-watered garden, like a spring whose waters never fail." That tells us that failures are okay, because God will turn them around into good things. They may not be our things, but they're *good* things. Nobody breaks out to win it. We just break out. But there's another one tomorrow, and the next day and the next. At least until Jesus comes back. Then it will just be a barrel roping!

The main thing is that we must have a relationship with Jesus in order to even have a chance at winning, breaking out or not. If you haven't found a living, vibrant relationship with him, I encourage you to make that decision, today. The runs won't be all record setters. As a matter of fact, we'll still miss here and there. But through it all, there is peace and life to the fullest. That's a life that can only be found through Jesus Christ. He is the way, the truth, and the life.

Great Challenges

We tend to romanticize the past.

In reality, it's a silly trick our minds seem to play on us that paint our yesterdays with beautiful colors. The pain and the stench disappear while the beauty stays. It doesn't matter if the past consists of riding thirteen miles of uphill Wallowa Mountain country to get to school in the freezing cold, we will often remember the beauty of the white blanket of snow and forget about the stabbing pain of the frostbitten toes beneath our Brogan shoes.

The Great Depression held so much pain, starvation, and hopelessness for so many, it's almost impossible to paint those pictures with any beauty at all. Furthermore, any attempts to do so are liable to be ridiculed by those who actually lived through those trying times. However, I have spent so much time with so many who did indeed live through those years, that I can't help believe that beauty indeed rose from the ashes.

My Grandpa Gooding always said they didn't really notice the Great Depression. They were poor country folk to begin with, and they had lived off the land for generations. Therefore, they were well fed during those same moments that others, much hungrier, were marching to Washington singing the "Battle Hymn of the Republic." Grandpa Campbell never remembered much different. Hard work had been a way of life for that entire generation, and they were amongst a nation full of Americans who all believed they could and would work their way out of the hole and into the light.

A World War employed and rebuilt a nation. Its soldiers returned home with a belief in an America that held hope and prosperity if they would only work for it. Some built businesses. Others built fence. Most built families and opportunities for their children, answering the timeless question, "Will things be better for my kids than they were for me?" with a definite yes.

Our founding fathers committed high treason in the name of freedom, and our grandfathers simply worked sunup to sundown, believing in a dream that was by no means free for the taking. The shot would cost them a great deal, everything as a matter of fact. But they were willing to sacrifice and serve—through a theatre of carnage during the most deadly war in human history and then through hard work and dedication to a job that would build homes, build schools, build communities, and ultimately rebuild a nation.

That generation had lived through need. They knew what it was to have nothing, and they knew what it took to change the situation. My grandparents taught their children to work, and their children taught us. But I think something has gone amiss in handing those skills down through the generations. As our nation grew, our affluence did, too. Dreams seemed to come true for my generation without the overhanging challenges of a depression and a World War. We never had to build a nation, simply take the digitized version of the ball and run with it. We've seen so much more and done so much more without having to sacrifice near as much as our grandparents, and the effect of that continues to increase exponentially with each passing year.

You can't find a kid on a pea combine these days. When my brother and I were young, we spent twelve hours a day, seven days a week sucking chaff down our shirts. When my grandfather ran a pea viner, he had already witnessed the fall of Nazi Germany with his own eyes. When my other grandfather began running the ranch on which he'd been raised, he had already left home to buckaroo, served for the cause in the Pacific Theatre, and lived more life than I have in forty years.

I know it's silly to say those were the good old days. I don't wish a war or a Great Depression on anyone. I do, however, wonder if some good came from those challenges. I know we have challenges, today, but it seems that when you're trying to drag your badly wounded buddy out of harm's way; when you're setting chokers on a horse logging operation just to have enough money to survive; when your biggest luxury was a fireside chat with the President via a crackly tube radio—it seems different things take top priority. All of the sudden a slow barista doesn't seem so bad after all. Not enough likes on a Facebook post doesn't even enter the picture. The score at the ball game is simply that—the score at the ball game.

I think when we have to go through times that take their toll from our hide, we grow. Howard Macey said, "The spiritual life cannot be made suburban. It is always frontier, and we who live in it must accept and even rejoice that it remains untamed." There is something about the frontier that brings the best out in people. Soldiers learn true love by laying their lives down for others, simply because they know that the others would do the same for them. When the hurricanes hit and take out metropolises, servants come out of the woodwork. Great deeds come from the greatest of challenges.

"Consider it pure joy, my brothers, whenever you face trials of many kinds, because you know that the testing of your faith develops perseverance. Perseverance must finish its work so that you may be mature and complete, not lacking anything." (James 1:2-4)

Bull Testing

"Them bulls'll hook ya."

Although that's one of my favorite lines from *Lonesome Dove*, when Pea Eye Parker and Gus McRae are considering chasing a herd of buffalo for the fun of it, it is also a pretty good warning in general. My friend Chris Grimes can attest to that as of late.

Will Rogers used to say, "All I know is what I read in the papers." I'll say, "All I know is what Dave Grimes told me." I confess, both sources can be questionable at times, but since Dave is fairly close to his son's goings on, I believe he can be considered a viable source. As with most good wrecks, if the storyteller is both close to the situation and laughing about it, the outcome must have required very little hospitalization.

Chris took a job not long ago working for Rob Thomas, running a herd of cows in Hermiston, Oregon. He loves it. After years of working in a feedlot, a little time in a few pastures has been a refreshing change for him. Of course, the primary purpose of the operation is producing seedstock, or in layman's terms, bulls and heifers to serve as the moms and dads in other producers' herds.

Running a seedstock operation requires a great deal of knowledge about cattle in general, and that herd in particular. Genetics is key, as is performance. Having a grasp on expected progeny differences in areas such as birth weight, calving ease, weaning weight, yearling weights, milking ability, etc. is just business as usual. Of course, when selling bulls, motility and viability in the bull's seed is crucial for reproduction and therefore critical for a producer to know.

In order to come up with that knowledge, certain tests become necessary. The main part of that test is what is lovingly referred to as collection, an intrusive procedure regardless of species. That portion of testing is what got Chris into his predicament.

They had just semen tested a bunch of bulls out at the Top Cut feedlot in Hermiston. Chris happened to be sorting off a bull, on foot, in the alley. The bull was making his way toward Chris, and he rattled his paddle at the animal, fully expecting him to slow down and turn into the open gate that was waiting on him. Chris' calculations were a bit off. The bull kept coming, and he was on the hunt.

It didn't take Chris long to figure out that he'd better find an escape route. He grabbed a fence rail and began to climb. Although his effort was valiant, it was a bit too little too late. The bull got his head underneath Chris' legs and flipped him over the fence into another pen full of bulls who had just been intruded upon. Their demeanor was less than cordial, and Chris told Dave the last thing he remembers was flying through the air.

Apparently, the bulls in that pen took turns camping out on Chris. Walt Sullivan called Dave and said, "I don't know how to tell you this, but I guess the good news is that Chris was conscious by the time they loaded him in the ambulance." After some listening, Dave finally discovered that his son had been mauled pretty good. Several staples in his head, a good strawberry on his cheek, and a jaw swelled the size of a softball became testament to the fight he had put up, or at least had been a part of that day.

Dave said they made it to the hospital in Hermiston to get Chris busted out. They took him home to help him heal up. Rob Thomas told Chris to take it easy for a day or two.

The next day, Dave and Chris went for a drive. Dave had some errands to run, but Chris looked at him and told him to drive out to the cows. They did. Chris checked salt, fed a little, and got some chores done, even though he looked and felt like he'd just been thrown under a runaway wagon. By the time they got home, Donna wondered where in the world they had been. Just at work, they told her. No big deal.

That's kind of the cowboy way. Sore, beat to a pulp, staples, stiches, and large pockets of fluid are not enough to keep him from getting the chores done. He might move a little more slowly, but he's still moving.

Those critters need him, and he'll do whatever it takes to make sure that they get taken care of, even if they *did* just try to kill him.

Wouldn't it be nice if our commitment to each other were that strong. The Bible says, "I'll show you my faith by what I do." I think a lot of the time, I spend too much time talking and not enough time doing. If I have to fight through blood and hardship to help someone out, and I come through, wouldn't that show more love than just preaching to them? That's the example Jesus set for us, anyway.

James 2:16-17 says, "If one of you says to him, 'Go, I wish you well; keep warm and well fed,' but does nothing about his physical needs, what good is it? In the same way, faith by itself, if it is not accompanied by action, is dead." When we actually do something to *show* our love instead of just saying it, then we're living like Jesus showed us.

Diane and the Hot Wire

Anyone who has spent time around critters of any kind has had at least some experience with electric fences. My Uncle Bob used to run a lot of cows on corn circles around Othello, Washington, and stringing a couple of hot wires around those winter pastures was commonplace. The first time I ran a cutting torch was as a little kid cutting the ends off of spud digger chains to build posts for those corn circles.

The problem with being around electric fences a lot is that one eventually finds him or herself in contact with one of those wires at some point. It is not a pleasant experience, but if I were a critter, it would definitely keep me in. That's the good part about a hot wire. The bad part about a hot wire is that they sneak up on you, kind of like a rattlesnake with no rattles.

Every time I've been hit by a hot wire, it feels like somebody has just hit me on the shoulder with a hammer. I find myself yelling out loud and reeling as if I've just taken an uppercut. Of course, some fencers hit a little harder than others, but ours will knock you back a few feet. I remember the first time our donkey checked that fence out. I watched it arc about an inch to pop him on the end of the snout, and he never came close to it again.

My Aunt Diane was cleaning out a water trough last summer. That should have been the toughest part of her day. She had left the water in it, and she was just cleaning some of the gunk out of it. The trough straddled two pastures, and the hot wire that ran through the pasture was routed just over the trough, along the boards that divided it in two. As she cleaned away, scrubbing like a barnyard Cinderella, she got completely lost in her work.

As she pulled her head out of the trough, however, her state of mind quickly changed. The back of her head came to rest on the live wire, and when it pulsed, it bit hard! She said it felt like a two by four hitting her across the neck, and she was forced hard and fast forward into the water trough. In a second, she was under water, still trying to figure out what had happened. By the grace of God, she missed the wire when she pulled herself out of the trough. She sat there in the pasture, putting the pieces of the puzzle together and realizing what had all transpired. Lesson learned. Turn the fencer off when cleaning the water trough.

I won't even come close to an electric fence, anymore. We have several testers, because I am not about to touch a hot wire with a blade of grass just to see if it's hot. I used to, but there comes a time when a guy just decides he doesn't like being shocked anymore. Maybe I'm scared, but I prefer to believe I've learned my lesson. Think it through to the outcome, and decide if it's worth it.

Many times, I've been tempted to do any number of things. Things that kind of sound like they might be fun, and maybe even harmless. Then I think it through. I realize what the consequences will be, and I change my mind. I realize who might be hurt, and I back off. I realize how it will separate me from God or the good he wants for me, and I turn around and go the other way.

It's kind of like checking a fence. I can grab the wire, or I can think it through and end up grabbing my tester. 1 Corinthians 3:19 says, "For the wisdom of this world is foolishness in God's sight." Thinking through the choices in our life with God's will foremost in our heart will help us make the right choices. Choices that don't dump our heads in the water. Wisdom will indeed keep us on the right side of the wire.

The Round Barn

On winter days, or even early spring days, when the wind is sucking right across these foothills in which I live, I'd really love to have Pete French's round barn in my backyard. Located just north of Diamond, Oregon and southeast of Crane, the round barn has become a landmark amongst the craters, rims, and sagebrush. The amazing thing is that it's been sitting out there in the middle of the desert, surviving floods, famines and presidents of both political parties for 130-some years. It's made of juniper posts and lava rock, and it's the perfect spot to start colts in the Great Basin winters.

Pete French's buckaroos were some handy builders in addition to their abilities with horses. The center of the barn is a stone circle, the middle of which held stalls that housed the winter's projects. A couple of doorways allow entry to the middle barn, and windows allow horses and cowboys alike to see in or out. Outside of the rock stable is a track around which buckaroos were able to lope horses. There's a board and batten wall around most of it, with one side wide open for good ventilation. The barn would be just as welcome in any modern day training facility as it was then.

If a person stands at the round barn and looks around, it's pretty obvious that trees have never been plentiful in that particular neck of the brush. Regardless of its scarcity of lumber, however, this portion of the French Glenn cattle empire played home to an edifice made up largely of massive juniper posts, milled boards, split shakes, and rough sawn boards and bats. The builders' dedication caused them to bring lumber from 60 miles north of the round barn's home, and the work of art is still sitting there to this day.

In that part of the country, a person can find more than one barn held up with junipers, and some of those posts have been in the ground well over a hundred years. Knowing that, I've cut many a juniper post and planted them, but most of mine have rotted off in a short period of time. My grandpa told me they had to be dry when I planted them. I've tried that, and I've been only slightly more successful. The key to a strong and long lasting post, like the ones found in the round barn of Pete French, is the heart.

Those buckaroos were not only able to find big junipers, they were able to find big junipers with red hearts. The red heart, according to the old timers, is what separates a hundred year old juniper post from a rotten two year old juniper post. The red heart is resistant to everything: bugs, rot, water, cats, and ugly dogs. The yellow outside will go away, but that strong heart will stay intact, and if a builder buries it deep enough, the post will stand the test of time. It's hard to say that for most other trees, but that round barn outside of Crane, Oregon is a testament to a strong heart.

God has put that kind of a heart into us. Jeremiah tells us our heart is evil. Jesus tells us something different. In Luke 6, he tells us, "The good man brings good things out of the good stored up in his heart, and the evil man brings evil things out of the evil stored up in his heart. For out of the overflow of his heart his mouth speaks." He's not telling us we haven't fallen short of the glory of God. He's telling us that he's here to make our hearts good again. Romans 5 goes on and on about how Jesus has made us righteous and at peace with him. With him, our hearts are good again.

That good heart, when planted, will last forever and bear good fruit. That good heart can only come through trusting in Jesus. Hebrews 11 talks about how we can't get there without faith, and that faith can only be in Jesus. Any heart without Jesus is like a yellow juniper. It will be rotten and thrown on the firewood pile in a couple of years (if not sooner). Our hearts can be good, but only through the only perfect heart that ever walked the earth.

The Two Pull Method

Many people do not comprehend the allure of the sagebrush country. To them, it's a desolate no-man's land inhabited by jackrabbits and cows. To me, it's got its own siren song that calls me back, and I go whenever I get a chance. I always dreamed of working on those big outfits. I never got to work on any of them, but I've helped a lot of guys in that country, and I came to realize that a twenty mile circle is a twenty mile circle. It's fun.

Those ranches intrigue me. The IL, the Roaring Springs, the Alvord, the Spanish Ranch and the MC have always pulled me in like a ship into the rocks. The people are every bit as cool as the country. They're a bit tougher than the average hand. They can't be afraid of rough horses or rough country, and they definitely can't be afraid of long days.

Jim Andrae, the IL's manager talked about the toughness required on the IL. He said they start their horses using the *two pull* method. "Pull up your latigo, and pull down your hat." I like it. Of course, I'm less fond of that method than I would have been twenty years ago, but sometimes, it just takes climbing on, not waiting for everything to be perfect.

Out on that desert, that's the way it is. I remember one time we were getting ready to ride out to move some cows on the Norman Ranches. Dally Taylor climbed on a horse of his, and that sucker put his head between his legs. Dally just rode him on over toward the gate while the horse was bucking. He rode him on out the gate and toward the cows while the horse continued to honk around. It didn't bother Dally at all. He had work to do.

Anyone who has long trotted for a lot of miles knows it takes toughness. On those big old famous ranches, the only way a guy can cover the country he needs to in a day is to trot. For some, that makes sore knees, sored legs, and sore horses. Those buckaroos on those ranches can't have horses that can't take it. The ranches can't have buckaroos that can't take it.

The day starts while it's dark down there, and for good reason. Cattle work better when it's cool. Horses work better when it's cool. However, that doesn't mean they only work in the cool. They work long days that end in the twilight, and sleep is a luxury.

The *two pull* method is great. It means that sometimes, we just have to take a leap and climb on. Maybe he won't buck at all. Maybe he'll buck us off. That's the same as life. If we wait and wait until all the conditions are perfect, we'll never jump. Think of how many times we pray for guidance on the same thing, just hoping we're hearing God right. "Should I take this job?" Sure, if you feel God's calling you to it. If he's not, you'll know, and it will all work out. But what if it's the perfect spot for you in sharing God's kingdom and you look too long without leaping? Some folks miss out.

When Gideon put his fleece out, he was showing a lack of faith. He should have just jumped when the angel told him what the deal was. He should have just charged out and conquered in God's name, knowing that God had told him that was the deal. But he didn't, and he'll always be remembered for a lack of faith. Pull up your latigo, and pull down your hat. That's how great things get accomplished.

"The apostles said to the Lord, 'Increase our faith!' He replied, 'If you have faith as small as a mustard seed, you can say to this mulberry tree, "Be uprooted and planted in the sea," and it will obey you.'"—Luke

WARBEX

We spent Saturday working cattle. My dad, Parker, Crae and I not only worked at getting the cows in, but we also spent a little time training horses, cows and kids. It was a good thing. By the time it was said and done, though, we were all pretty tired: horses, cows and kids. Regardless, between the blood, the needles, pocketknives and wormer, we ended up having a pretty darned good day and very few injuries and or temper tantrums.

I don't mind giving shots, and castrating bull calves isn't all that bad, either, but I hate worming cattle. The main reason is that I tend to get it on me nearly every time. I will guarantee you that I am not going to be packing any horn flies any time soon. But I don't think it's entirely healthy to get a whole lot of that on you in any way, shape, or form. We usually have those jugs where you squeeze the wormer up into the graduated cup and just pour it on. Unfortunately, they always leak—always. Once in a while, I'll wear rubber gloves, but then I get to doing something else, a cow needs wormed, and I just grab the wormer and start squeezing, and by the time I think about putting on gloves, it's already on my hands.

Ivermectin is a little better to get on your hands than other products that have come down the pike, though. Most anyone who has been around the cattle business has been exposed to Warbex and its odiferous and potent properties. That stuff will kill any kind of critter crawling around in a cow, and it's a miracle it doesn't kill the cow, herself. We used to sell it by the boatload every spring at the feed store, and it always came with a free dipper. Just pour the Warbex in a bucket and dip away. Warbles be danged.

And anything smaller than 300 pounds with which that stuff came into contact was in for a world of hurt. My buddy Dally Taylor told me about a place down around Diamond where they were working cows, and the bucket got spilled. Unfortunately, a border collie dog happened to be lying under the catwalk on which the bucket was sitting, and in a matter of minutes, the dog was dead. The stuff would attack the heart tissue and brain tissue as soon as it went through the system. That happened pretty quickly because of the solvent in it. The poison was in and through a small critter pretty quickly. Another story I heard, albeit third hand, told of an old guy who spilled a bunch of it on himself while they were working cows out in the middle of nowhere, and he let it go until he had gotten really sick that evening. By the time they got him to town, he had died.

That's some potent stuff, used to do a good thing, like take care of some bugs in cattle. When it's used in the proper dosages, it's pretty useful, but when a critter gets too much, the critter is gone. There are a lot of drugs like that. There's only so much you can let get into you, before it becomes toxic.

The world's like that, too. We have to live in it, so we have to do things like pay taxes, follow speed limits, wear clothes, celebrate birthdays, pay for prom dates, and all that stuff. However, we are admonished to be *in* the world, not *of* the world. 1 John 2:15-17 tells us, "Don't love the world's ways. Don't love the world's goods. Love of the world squeezes out love for the Father. Practically everything that goes on in the world—wanting your own way, wanting everything for yourself, wanting to appear important—has nothing to do with the Father. It just isolates you from him. The world and all its wanting, wanting, wanting is on the way out—but whoever does what God wants is set for eternity." (*The Message*)

Holy cow! Was John at a rodeo when he wrote that? Never mind. The point is that when we love the world and its ways, it squeezes out love for the Father. I know that from experience. I hate to admit it, but there've been times in my life where I've approached God and had to say, "Remember me, Jesus?" That's bad. That's like spilling Warbex on yourself. It goes right to the heart and mind and it changes you, and it's not for the good. You bet we've got to live here, but Jesus can still be our number one priority. Do we need to live in mud huts in Africa? Not at all, unless that's what we're called to, but we surely need to give our desires to Jesus. Then he'll take them and give them right back to us in ways we've never dreamed.

RANCH WIVES

Cowboy romance is somewhat of an oxymoron, but it does exist. As a matter of fact, it is evident every spring when the strong, brave rancher straddles his horse to rope and drag calves to the fire while his eight month pregnant wife is on the ground, flanking them, branding them, vaccinating them, and whittling on their *cojones*. Ranch wives have the fortitude of a soldier. They get yelled at, run over, left behind, and once in a while, they get flowers.

Ranch wives who grew up on a ranch are prepared for the life they sign onto when he places the ring on her hand. However, those who come from a gentile background (they grew up in town) are generally in for a rude awakening. The tough ones embrace the life and praise God for the challenging adventure. The rest either leave, run their husband over with a tractor, or begin drinking heavily. My friend, Lindsay Murdock, is the former.

Lindsay did not grow up around ranching, and at one point she had created visions of a strong, brave rancher coming to sweep her off her feet. Instead, she got Ian. That came with the typical stress-filled life of a rancher husband who's up all hours of the night during calving; cutting hay when the family should be camping with the folks from church; and needing her to drive when he's feeding cows in the winter. The romance wore off fairly quickly for Lindsay.

She's driven kinds of equipment she never knew existed. She's carried one end of raising two boys into ranch life. She's learned how to pull calves, give shots, and change pipe. She's basically had a baptismal under fire into the 'round the clock life of ranching and farming, and she loves it. That's actually an understatement. She embraces the life with her whole heart and her whole being. She photographs it. She writes about it, and she praises God for it.

To see her enthusiasm for *real* ranch life is inspiring. Lindsay doesn't over-romanticize her life, whatsoever, and with humility, she stands by Ian through the good times and the loud ones. I love reading her writing and looking at her photographs of a life that never makes the headlines. Few television westerns even come close to getting it right. When Ian pulls her out of bed in the middle of the night for help, she still has to get up and go teach school in the morning. Nevertheless, she's right there.

A lot of ranch wives embrace the life, despite its inherent difficulties. My wife is tough enough to leave me to work by myself, if I don't behave. Other wives take over the operations after a husband's death. Some are the right hand man to a workaholic husband who may have a hard time keeping up with her. Ranch wives are impressive.

One of the things I admire about Lindsay, however, is the way she is able to take the most mundane aspects of ranch life, and make them appear to be the biggest blessings from God. The slightest gifts become gold to her, and that's a tough thing for a lot of ranch wives, especially those who didn't grow up in the life. She's truly thankful for the opportunity to live the crazy life of a nursemaid to a herd of black bally cattle.

I think what helps her embrace the ranching lifestyle is her faith in where God is leading her in life. She knows he's placed her right where she is, and to her, that's exciting. That's the way it should be for all of us. Regardless of how plain Jane and mundane our lives might appear to the "American Idol" crowd, they truly are rich with blessings. Even when we're being shaken out of bed in the middle of the 2:00 a.m. check, there's good in the situation. Romans 8:28 tells us, "And we know that in all things God works for the good of those who love him, who have been called according to his purpose." I think being a ranch wife is a calling that serves a purpose greater than even any rancher can fathom. When one of them embraces that calling the way Lindsay does, it does nothing but bring glory to the one who called her there.

JJ AND THE KIDS

As a rodeo announcer, I've been the butt of a few clowns' jokes. It's okay. Humilitation, I guess, is part of the job. A while back, I worked with my friend JJ Harrison, and he definitely took his liberties at making fun of me throughout the performances. As a barrelman who has worked the NFR, he doesn't hold much back, but it was all in fun.

However, he told me a story that leads me to believe that what goes around comes around.

JJ had just finished working the Reno Rodeo and had pointed his motorhome northwest toward St. Paul, Oregon for the Fourth of July rodeo there. Unfortunately, getting out of Reno isn't entirely easy during early summer, and JJ found himself stopped in gridlocked traffic on the freeway. As he sat at the helm of his motorhome, he passed the time by staring through the windshield at the lines of non-moving cars ahead of him.

As his impatience grew, JJ was interrupted by a knock at his door. He opened it to see a lady and her children. "Excuse me, sir. My little boy needs to use the restroom really bad. Can he use yours?"

JJ was caught off guard. He wondered if she was serious. I mean, what if the traffic were to start moving? "Please, sir. We'll hurry." JJ decided to oblige the panicked mother.

He opened the door and let her and her three children in. He showed her to the bathroom, and she took the full-up child to do his business. As the boy was in the latrine, the traffic began to move. "Um, ma'am, the traffic's moving," he nervously told the woman. In a panic, she jumped out the door and headed for her car, leaving her children behind in the flabbergasted rodeo clown's motorhome. The traffic indeed began to move.

JJ drove forward at a snail's pace, wondering what to do. Soon, it sank in that he was indeed driving down the freeway with three children he did not know, whose mother was in a car somewhere on the freeway, he hoped was close to him. The fear began to set in. JJ wondered, "What if this traffic really breaks loose?" He began to freak out.

He looked in the rearview mirror at two confused children. JJ didn't even know their names. Would he have to take them all the way to St. Paul? Would she try to follow, or were the children wards of the clown? For a rare moment, JJ Harrison had nothing to say.

Soon, traffic began to slow. Hope filled the barrelman's heart. In a matter of seconds, the motorhome had come to a complete stop. The child in question poked his head out of the bathroom, and in seconds, their mother arrived for their retrieval. JJ breathed out a huge sigh of relief.

As JJ told the story, I thought it was funny. He did, too, although I'm fairly certain that at the time he was sure he was stuck in a nightmare. Imagine, though, the thoughts going through those kids' heads. They had no clue with whom they were traveling. For all they knew, he was a psycho, not a clown. Regardless, after the traffic started moving, the ride had begun.

Sometimes, God leads us into places in which we feel very uncomfortable. The panic sets in. We don't know who's traveling with us. We don't know how things are going to end up, but we have to keep moving forward. That's the part so many of us don't really like about following Jesus. It makes us feel uncomfortable. We panic when we don't know how it's all going to end.

I heard someone say once, "There's no growth in a comfort zone, and there's no comfort in a growth zone." I think that's the truth. If God were going to call us into places where we felt comfortable all the time, how would we grow? We wouldn't, and our faith would grow stale, and we'd become flabby believers, or as one writer calls them, "practical agnostics."

Proverbs 3:5-6 tells us, "Trust in the Lord with all your heart, and lean not on your own understanding; in all your ways acknowledge him, and he will make your paths straight." Trusting God is easy when everything's looking like we planned it. But that's not trusting God. Trusting God is more like driving down the freeway with a motorhome full of some stranger's kids and knowing they'll be returned eventually. We can't be scared of being uncomfortable.

Even Keeled

I've discovered that junior rodeo parents, at least on the roughstock end of the arena, are all liars. I would have to include myself in that statement, I suppose. But it's kind of funny to see kids climbing on and watching their parents lie to them.

Of course there are different extremes of lying. There's the boy who absolutely did not want to nod his head on his steer. He was crying and begging his dad not to make him nod. I told him he looked just like a PBR guy (that wasn't a lie; they won't nod, either). Then I told him that we'd catch him. I amended my statement almost as quickly as it came out of my mouth. I told him we'd *try* to catch him. Still, that was a lie. I didn't really try very hard.

Then there was the kid who was wanting to get on but was a little nervous. His dad was standing there telling him, "Oh, this one's the nice one. He just hops out there. Just a high loper." The kid asked what a high loper was. I asked which rodeo he had been watching. Every one of those steers bucked and bucked hard. I don't think there was a high loper in the bunch.

Then there was the parent who said, "It won't hurt at all. That dirt's nice and soft." He was right. The dirt was nice and soft. However, when steers buck you off and then step on you, when they fill your helmet with so much dirt you can't breathe, then some issues begin to arise about the definition of the word *hurt*.

There was another dad who kept telling his son, "Man, you got this." His son hadn't ever been on anything before, and those steers were firing. I don't think *Dad* would have "had this."

Ultimately, though, the biggest lie was about how nice the steers were. They weren't nice. They bucked. My son was well aware of that, and he wasn't the least bit scared. He just stood there chewing on his mouthpiece, waiting his turn. When they ran his steer in, I lied. "Ooooh. You've got the good one, buddy." I don't think he even heard me. He was trying to get his rope on him. I saw my lying wasn't going to do any good, so I just let him go about his business and let him tell me what he needed from me.

He's gotten past the point of needing to be lied to. He was watching kid after kid get piledrived after their dads had told them they had hoppers. He knew they were going to buck, and it didn't seem to bother him. Why, I thought, should I continue lying to him about it?

Crae kind of adheres to basketball coach Denny Crum's ideas on getting psyched up and trying to talk oneself into being ready for competition. Coach Crum says, "I don't try to get players emotionally up for a game; it creates too many peaks and valleys. I strive for even keel; they will get up for the big games." Even keel. We could all take a lesson from guys like Coach Crum and my son. Don't get me wrong. My son doesn't walk on water. As a matter of fact, I just got done punishing him for whining and throwing a baby fit. However, he's got some things figured out I wish I had had figured out when I was crawling on buckers.

Regardless of whether a horse (or a steer) bucks out his hind end or just gently jumps and kicks, you do the same thing. You make the same moves, lift on your rein the same, hustle your feet the same. Whatever. The guys that realize that don't need talked into anything. I used to have to talk myself into riding well a lot of the time. It wasn't that I didn't want to get on. It was that I had a lack of confidence. Crae lacks that confidence on the timed event end of the arena, but on the roughstock end, he knows his job doesn't change, regardless of what they run under him.

And that's why I realized I didn't need to blow sunshine up his nose and lie to him about how big of a creampuff his steer was. It didn't matter to him. He did his job, and so did the steer. The steer would have bucked off most grown men. Crae got bucked off hard, got up, grabbed his rope and put his stuff away. He didn't get mad or happy. He was just matter-of-fact about the whole deal. He felt good about his effort, and that comes only from confidence. Confidence comes only from knowing the truth about the situation and knowing you're ready to do your part.

It's a lot like our walk with God. When we know the truth, we don't have to talk ourselves into things by lying to ourselves. We know our part. We know we need to love others, and there doesn't need to be a reward for us. We don't need to get a feel-good fuzzy feeling out of the deal. We just do it. That goes for anything. Even keel is good. God promised us he'd never leave us nor forsake us, so we don't have to talk ourselves into believing he is present. He is. Whether we *feel* like it, or not. He tells us so. Plain and simple.

Proverbs 17:27 says, "A man of knowledge uses words with restraint, and a man of understanding is even-tempered." We don't have to rattle off a bunch of Christian sounding stuff to be Christians. We just need to say what needs to be said and nothing more. When we allow our lives to be filled with peaks and valleys, highs and lows, and have to talk ourselves into loving or serving God, it rattles us. God's always here, and we can and are called to be even keeled. Plain and simple.

Old Tack Rooms

Several years back, we went to a concert a cowboy singer was putting on at a pretty well-known establishment. I'm fairly certain everyone we knew was there, so the event was truly a reunion of sorts. As the cowboy singer was getting ready to take the stage, people from all over the Northwest caught up on old times, horses they'd been riding, cows they'd sold and everything else they could come up with to both reminisce and share the latest.

As the master of ceremonies began to introduce the cowboy singer, he spun a yarn about the beauty of growing up on a ranch. His descriptions of the ranch life of a growing boy a half century earlier were idyllic. He told of the hardships in a way that made them seem nearly fun. Then he began to lament the loss of his grandfather's tack room. Those were the memories that truly lived in his heart and that had brought him to where he was that very night.

The emcee wove a tapestry of his grandfather's tack room that shared with us a picture of well-built saddles, bridles organized neatly upon hooks on the wall, and the aroma of newly oiled leather. He shared with us, the audience, the sounds of creaking saddles as they were gently slid onto their stands and the softness of the saddle blankets and pads as they were placed on top of the saddles to dry. He lamented, "I'll never forget the smell of my grandfather's tack room. The strong smell of that leather and horse will always bring a smile to my heart."

The description was indeed a work of art. We were nearly caught up into the rapture of the moment with him. My brother, however, was sitting at a table with our friend Jim Ward. Jim added his recollections to the description, albeit unheard by the emcee. "Leather and horse? Man, all my grandpa's tack room smelled like was wet dogs and mouse pellets." Leave it to Jim to bring a little bit of reality to the romantic description!

However, that really is the truth. The years may color the memories a little bit, but when that reality is the day in and day out of a person's real life, the aromas stink a little more. The beautiful cedar tongue and groove walls of the tack room turn into the torn up OSB walls of the vet shack, branded with everyone in the county's iron. Mud three inches deep and twenty years old and scale tickets from countless loads of cattle might round it out. The dewy spring mornings with birds singing and calves bounding get replaced with 3:30 a.m. weigh-ins of fat cattle and foggy-headed cowboys trying to shake loose the cobwebs and get a read on where they are.

Perhaps the sweet smell of rolled oats gets replaced by the dead mouse you find in your grain scoop. The quiet morning in the saddling shed turns into a pulling back bronc who stands on your frostbit foot on that quaint wooden floor. The aroma of bacon and eggs turns into the pound on the door at 2:30 telling you it's time to eat. The cowboy hat, shotgun chaps, and Paul Bond boots gets replaced by a goofy looking Scotch cap, three layers of sweatshirts, a pair of wet gloves, Carhart coveralls, and a pair of five buckles.

The life usually looks a little better in memories, paintings, and Sam Elliott westerns. But that doesn't mean the real life doesn't have its rewards. There truly is joy in hardship. It's just harder to find. I remember watching my six-year-old son nurse a sick calf all night. He was right there helping from the time that calf was born until the little booger died in the middle of the night. I remember him getting up every couple of hours, putting his coat on over his pajamas, his little Stormy Kromer hat on his head, and a pair of gloves on his hands just to go make sure that calf lived. And when he walked into that barn and found that little, black calf dead in the corner of the stall, I remember the tears and the heartache. But I also remember seeing him grow just a little bit.

That's what real life does for us. We sure don't need to be thankful for dead mice in the grain can or two below weather during calving season. But take a look around. Would you rather be anywhere else? I love what 1

Thessalonians 5:16-18 says. It tells us, "Be joyful always, pray continually, give thanks in all circumstances; for this is God's will for you in Christ Jesus." When we figure out how to do that, we truly have found the life Jesus died and rose again to give us.

Outsmarting the Wild Ones

Jess Wenick is an ecologist. Anyone who has a question about the range and its relationships with cattle, humans and wildlife can ask Jess, and he'll have the answer. He's also Harney County born and bred. For anyone outside of Oregon, that means he's got a little desert rat and a lot of cow in him. I first got to know Jess when we were going to school together at Eastern Oregon University. Looking at him from across the ag lounge, one wouldn't guess him as a Harney County boy. He didn't look punchy enough. A farmer, maybe, but not a buckaroo.

I was proven wrong. We were gathering cows down around Burns, and Jess showed up to ride. Although he had grown up on the desert and knew cows and cow country, he wasn't entirely interested in looking the part. He showed up in a ball cap, and that trickled right on down to his lace up work boots, to which he had taped a pair of spurs. The boots were so big that the spurs wouldn't really fit, so he grabbed some duct tape and fastened them on. To say the least, Jess definitely looked more like a range ecologist than a range rider.

The boss thought it would be funny to give him a little scare, too. He told him, "Jess, we cut out the rankest horse in the herd for you. That sucker works like clockwork, though. At seven a.m., sharp, every day, that horse will go to bucking. Be ready."

Truth be known, the horse was as much of a deadhead as an English professor, but Jess didn't know that. He trotted off a bit nervous about his mount, and we all kind of chuckled to ourselves a bit.

At noon, we'd gathered the cattle near a watering hole, and we spent the next hour sorting the neighbor's cows out of the bunch. Jess's horse worked great through it all. When we got done and the cattle were soaking a little, we all got off and uncinched our ponies. Somebody looked at Jess and said, "Well, you don't look like you got bucked off."

He looked at the rest of us and smiled. He had outsmarted the horse. Jess grinned like a cat as he said, "Well, I got the better end of him. I got off of him at a quarter 'til and led him around until about 7:15."

Isn't it funny how we get this picture in our head of what might happen and it causes us to do things as unimaginable as walk when we've got a perfectly good saddle horse at the end of our McCarty? We fear what is to come more than we ever should, so we sit there and shake and fear and make more work for ourselves than was ever necessary.

The Israelites did that when Goliath was calling them out. They were scared to death of one loud mouthed, blind Phillistine, and they were an entire army! None of them were willing to look beyond the appearance and see the reality, or at least risk a little on God. They were fine just leading their horse around for a half hour. Sure, it keeps you from getting bucked off, but when the horse is dog gentle to begin with, isn't it worth getting in tune with Jesus for a little truth?

1 Samuel tells us David had no problem riding through the storm. As a matter of fact, he didn't even perceive it as a storm, because God was on his side. Chapter 17 says, "David said to the Philistine, 'You come against me with sword and spear and javelin, but I come against you in the name of the Lord Almighty, the God of the armies of Israel, whom you have defied.'" He stepped out there in confidence, just like we need to do in all of the scary situations in our life. God is for us, and if that's the case, who can be against us?

I don't blame Jess for not wanting to get in a jackpot. We all laughed about it, and he even wrote about it later on. But if we can learn a lesson—to trust God through the toughest spots and step out in his name and in faith—we will be victorious even if the storm should actually arrive.

WINTER'S SONG

On a brisk night like this, it seems that God has littered the black sky with twice as many stars as usual. It's a different arrangement of constellations than I stare at on a summer night lying on the ground on a bedroll. Winter has begun to ratchet the dippers to different sections of the night air, and the beauty can be seen as clearly as a bull elk through a good spotting scope.

The coyotes are howling, yipping, and declaring the glory of God with a song that pierces through the cold air from miles off. Sound travels further on a night like this. The air is thin. It's cold, and it's almost as if those notes from the coyote choirs are sliding on ice toward my back porch. The only fog in the sky is that coming out of my mouth and my dog's nose. The beauty is amazing.

They don't get nights like this in town. Of course, they don't have to break ice twice a day, either. Their fingers don't sting after flaking bale after bale of oat hay and throwing it to a herd of cows. But then again, the beauty's a pretty good trade for a pair of rose tinted cheeks and frozen nose hairs. Whether it's morning or night, the magnificence of the brilliant sunshine defining every frost brushed blade of frozen grass and the clarity of a winter, night sky sing the same tune. They sing out God's glory.

I've always loved winter. I don't mind a little cold to challenge the day a bit. I remember days and weeks of riding through frozen corn circles and turnip fields with my Uncle Bob feeding cows, and every time the ground freezes, my mind and heart goes back there. I've always loved feeding. An extremely windy and wet morning might challenge that notion a little bit, but that's about it.

Calving is a joy, as well. Of course, by the end of a sixty to ninety day calving season, many ranchers might have the temperament of a tormented badger, but seeing a winter feed ground accented with baby calves cuts the edge off a bit. We've all shown up on those below freezing nights and had to shake the air into a calf's lungs or filled the calving shack with five or six newborns to keep them alive until morning. Every time they kick the door open on the camp trailer, the below zero bite wakes us from our shallow slumber. It's worth every minute.

I don't mind breaking ice. I don't mind calving heifers. I don't mind feeding. When the weather turns to Scotch cap-wearing temperatures, I'm right at home. That's my time of the year.

So as I stand on the porch, listening to a chamber choir of coyote sopranos, I am taken to a place of joy. Yes, there's work. There are challenges nearly insurmountable. There are annoyances. There are days that test the will of creatures to live. And it's wonderful. Those challenges—they're what brings the joy.

A good challenge is the patina on a life well-lived. Although he created us to live in constant fellowship and harmony with him, God never designed us for challenge-less existence. Once he created Adam, he gave him work to do. Our work gives us purpose. It gives us meaning. It is given by God, and it's a gift. Winter brings that with an innocence, a starkness, an intensity that is reserved only for those beautiful nights so cold that life seems to have exited the landscape with the exception of those coyotes and the man in the silk scarf listening to their song.

For many, winter is a time of emptiness, of lifelessness, of dormancy. For me, winter represents all that is true and powerful in God and what he has blessed us with to overcome any and all challenges. When we are faced with challenges, we are faced with opportunity. When we are faced with opportunity, we are rewarded with joy. Psalm 128 says, "You will eat the fruit of your labor; blessings and prosperity will be yours." In order to get there, we must labor. Despite its coldness and deadness, winter truly does bring fruit.

Cow Whisperers

The most interesting duo of cowmen I have ever seen was the father son team I had the fortune of rubbing elbows with while the guy for whom I worked calved a few of his heifers out in their feedlot. I like to call them—*the cow whisperers*.

Both of these gentlemen were scared to death of anything equine. To get either of them on a horse was like getting Hillary Clinton to climb on Bodacious. They had a healthy, almost phantasmagoric respect for the bovine species that prevented them from raising their voices, making any sudden movements, and/or moving toward the cattle in any conceivable way.

We were sorting off a few girls one afternoon to put out in a corn circle. I saw the ones that we needed to cut off, I had a good dog, and I had the trailer backed to the alley. All we needed was to peel the three mamas off of the back of the herd, move them the ten yards to the right place, shut the gate, and all would be done. I started to move into place. The old man raised his hand as he leaned on his ski pole. "Whoa," he whispered. "Don't spook 'em." His son looked like a clone standing on the other side of him.

I whispered back. I whispered back? "Okay, what's your plan?"

He answered earnestly, "Let's just watch 'em and see what they do." I had to give it a try. As Kenny Frazier said once, I might as well try to prove 'em wrong. We watched for what seemed like an eternity. The three cows I was after stayed where they were—standing off by themselves, calves on their sides, eating some hay. A black bally pooped. A small bird landed on the back of a cow. One old girl moved her off hind foot backwards one step. I thought the ball had finally dropped when that Hereford swished her tail! Almost sent me reeling backwards from the excitement.

After about twenty minutes of trying to cut these girls off telepathically, I went ahead and told the boys, "I've got to get going. This ain't getting us anywhere."

"No, wait!" whispered the dad. "She's moving." He pointed to the outside cow. Sure enough, she was moving. By the time she had laid all the way down to bask in the sun-warmed mud, I had almost lost my mind.

Their book should be coming out this summer, and their clinics are free. *Stress Free Husbandry: Working Cows Through Telepathy*. It ought to be a hit.

On the same note, don't we many times get impatient with God? I've learned over the years, that it's not a bad idea to sit back and let a cow find the gate on her own. Back then, I was ram and jam, and now I realize that causes just as many wrecks as it solves. Trusting God to do what he says he'll do is critical to success in our lives. And I'm not necessarily talking success in the world's terms. I'm talking success in seeing God's will for our lives come into play.

I'm like everyone else—maybe even worse. I want it right now. Jesus, I want your perfect plan to come right now. I want that blessing to come right now. I want this mountain to be thrown into the sea right now. But our God takes his time. We can't hurry God's will any more than we can successfully hurry a baby out of the womb. 2 Peter 3:9 says, "The Lord is not slow in keeping his promise, as some understand slowness. He is patient with you, not wanting anyone to perish, but everyone to come to repentance." Aren't you glad God takes it slow? As many times as it takes for us to get it right, we'd better pray for him to do that. Slow down, and trust God. It makes for a quicker time.

The Top of the Ridge

"Breakfast is at three," Gary Marshall said as he headed off to bed. The rest of us weren't in any hurry to hit the hay, but it's because we were like a bunch of kids at a slumber party. We hadn't seen each other in a while, and we were tickled to get to catch up on old times. Branding calves was the gravy, and the next day, we were to gather a 25,000 acre allotment and get ready for the day after's big serving.

Gary had gotten the map out a little earlier, and he showed us the plan. Each of us would take a corner, and we'd meet in the middle at the bottom of a juniper ridge in a kind of natural branding trap. If we could get all the cattle there, then we'd have a lot less gathering to get done on the big morning. The plan seemed pretty simple, and as I'd ridden out there before, I had it pretty well seared into my mind's eye.

We carried on for another hour or more, and then we figured we'd better hit the rack, or we weren't going to be able to get up by breakfast. Gary wasn't kidding when he said the grub was at three, and he'd often kid, "It don't take long to stay all night around here." That was for certain.

When we went to bed, Mandi expressed her concern to me. "What if I get lost? That's a lot of country." I felt bad for laughing at her. She was right; it was a lot of country, but it would be tough to get lost.

I told her, "If you get lost, ride to the top of the nearest ridge or hill, and you'll be able to see California from there. In between, you're bound to see someone you know." It didn't seem to calm her nerves much, but she'd see what I was talking about the next morning.

At three, we were sitting in the dining room. At four, we were saddling ponies. At five, most of us were sleeping in the rig on the way to Riley. By six, we had hit a long trot to our respective corners to start a black bally Easter egg hunt; and by noon, we were holding a rodear where the branding trap was set up. All of us were there, even Mandi. She hadn't gotten lost.

She had gotten into some pretty tall sagebrush, and so had the rest of us. There is seriously some sagebrush that's over a man's head, even when he's horseback. Nevertheless, if you ride to the top of a hill or ridge, you can see forever. That's just part of what I love about the desert. Can you get lost? You bet. But it ain't easy.

In reality, that's how God works, too. We get trucking along in life and get into some pretty thick brush, and we're just not quite sure where we are. At those times, we just need to get into God's presence—through his Word, conversations with him, or just quietness with him. When we do that, we can see a lot of stuff we couldn't see before. He makes our way a little bit more plain. We can't see every step, because there are a lot of ditches and chuckholes, even downed fences out there in that brush, but we can sure get a good glimpse at the right direction.

Jesus wants us to ride to the top of his ridge. We worry about getting lost, but we try to find our own way instead of just heading for him. Psalm 107 says, "Some wandered in desert wastelands, finding no way to a city where they could settle. They were hungry and thirsty, and their lives ebbed away. Then they cried out to the Lord in their trouble, and he delivered them from their distress." That's really all it takes for us to get a good view, just calling out to the Lord, giving him our attention instead of worrying about the tall sage and deep ravines. We can't get lost, folks. It's nearly impossible if we trot up the right hill.

Lonely Ticket Counters

Dyrk Godby is a rodeo renaissance man. In the olden days, he was a bronc stomper worth a pretty good pinch of salt. I would imagine what made him a good bronc peeler was his toughness. Put him in a boxing ring, and the other guy'd better have his hammer cocked. A broken neck slowed him down a little, and soon he turned to judging rodeos. Having grown up the son of a cowboy, though, rodeo was not where it ended for Dyrk. He was just as handy outside of the arena as he was climbing down into a bucking chute.

Beyond that, Dyrk has an artistic bent that scatters a couple of different ways. Anyone who has seen his artwork has witnessed some of rodeo's finest depictions. He's got a painting of a calf roper getting off and heading down the rope that is absolutely perfect. Moving out of the arena, he depicts horses, cattle, and mules with accuracy and passion. He's changed his medium lately by beginning to wood burn drawings into leather items such as briefcases and purses. In true cowboy fashion, his art has become utilitarian.

He can sing and write songs, as well. Whether those songs are about "feather-footed horses and a few barroom brawls" or about growing up cowboy, they paint just as good of picture as Dyrk's brushes do. A few years ago, he called me up and visited with me about songwriting and artwork, and after that, we'd exchange new songs once in a while. Of course, he bought most of the stamps; I write about one song every five years.

When a person takes all of his artwork into consideration, though, the reason it speaks so well is because it comes from a guy who knows his subject. One example of that is a painting that hangs on the wall of Bob Burkhart's art studio, just out of Bozeman, Montana. The painting depicts a lone cowboy in an empty airport leaning on a ticket counter. His bronc saddle is tied up at his feet, and his rigging bag isn't too far away. The sepia toned nature of the painting gives it that lonely-late-at-night feeling that way too many bronc stompers have seen from the hurricane deck. Like Bob says about the painting, we've all been there. We've got a good one drawn somewhere and can't get a ticket, or we've just fallen off somewhere, we're broke, and we just want to get home.

The painting is so stark. It's so simple. But it tells such a truth. We're always coming, or we're going. Sometimes, we're excited to get somewhere, and sometimes, we just want to go home. Regardless, it seems that so many times something gets thrown into the gears to keep that from happening. Perhaps it's sin. Maybe it's an enemy who simply wants to tear our souls to a state of doubt or unbelief. It could be our own stubbornness about "doing it my way". Regardless of what the cause might be, when we are standing alone just wanting to get somewhere—anywhere but here, we can tend to feel very alone.

The good news is that we're never alone. God's right there with us, and where it seems like there's no way, he'll make a way. I know he will, because he promises us. He may take us as far as we can possibly stretch, but sometimes that's what he wants from us—everything. Wouldn't it be nice if we would just stretch that far to begin with? Then, we might not end up at the lonely ticket counter just wanting to get somewhere.

When we fully obey God, when we fully give him our all, he'll bless us. According to Deuteronomy 28, "If you fully obey the Lord your God and carefully follow all his commands I give you today, the Lord your God will set you high above all the nations on earth. " Wouldn't it be nice to be set high instead of being stuck somewhere that makes us feel trapped? Let's reach as far as God has given us the ability, and we'll stay away from those lonely nights in the airport.

THE GOOD FIGHT

Ian Tyson says he likes old corrals and sagebrush. I have the same feelings. However, I think I'm just as fond of a new corral as I am of an old one.

I just drove from Casper, Wyoming to Prineville, Oregon. Some of the country through which I travelled is the most beautiful in the world, specifically the Jackson Hole. I don't think anyone could look at the Tetons and not think they're amazing. I'm pretty fond of the buffalo, the moose, and the elk I saw while traveling through there, as well. To stop and look out over the winding Snake River with the Tetons towering above is worth the time it takes.

The worst part about Jackson Hole is probably the town, even though it's pretty cool and western. As cool and western as it may be, it's a bit on the preppy side, and it panders to people who make a lot more money than I ever will. But those are the very people who can afford places around Jackson. As I drove West out of town, I began to pass by a lot of beautiful ranches, each with a magnificent mansion made out of log, stone, rough board, or some other rustic material. That's where rustic ended, though. Most of them were what I would guess at well over million dollar homes situated on some of the most beautiful ground one could find.

However, what I didn't see much of were corrals. I'm not talking about panel pens to hold a few horses; I'm talking about shipping pens that get used to gather, brand, and ship cattle. The more I thought about that, the more I realized that most of those magnificent homes were more than likely cabins for folks who stay while the staying's good then head back to their apartment in comfortable Chicago or San Francisco when the weather gets bad or the work begins to feel like work. When the going gets tough, the residents pack up and leave.

Further on in my travels, I reached some real ranch country, and I began to see corrals. I saw old ones, but I saw a lot of newer ones, too. Not a whole lot of fancy ones, but corrals built by ranchers who live a hard scrabble existence of working hard to make their places go. Those corrals not only represent a lifestyle; they represent a commitment to a life. They represent a devotion to sticking around regardless of how hard it gets, how bad the weather is, how many miles of fence need built, how many calves need pulled, or how many of the family have to get a job in town. Those folks are working that land and making it pay for itself.

They're not pulling up stakes just because they lose a month of sleep during calving season. They're not skinning out because they lost their hind end on a down market. They're committed, and they're staying. Why? That's just what you do. You don't quit just because of a little misery. You stick it out, because that's the life you've been called to. That's just the way it is.

Our daughter, Parker is beautiful. She loves to sing. She loves to decorate, and she absolutely loves going for walks. But she's had seizures nearly her entire life. In the past ten years, we've struggled, fought, screamed, prayed, and cried, hoping for a life without seizures for our little girl. People often say, "Man, I just don't know how you do it." That always blows our minds. What are we supposed to do? Quit? You just do it. That's all there is to it. I hate having to get up in the middle of the night and hold my daughter while she seizes. I hate that she doesn't do as well in school as the other kids her age. I hate that she can't talk as well or walk as well, but I am committed as a dad, and Mandi is committed as a mom.

Commitment is not something that goes away when the hard times come. That's not commitment at all. That's quitting. That's giving up. Whether that's in parenting, ranching, holding a marriage together, or keeping a ranch afloat during the dry times, commitment doesn't quit. It may beat its head against the wall. It may spend late nights screaming. It may spend months in despair. It may work so hard to see so little return that it wants to give up, but commitment *never* gives up.

We started Parker on a new medicine in the summer of 2013. We had tried everything. Everything. No results ever came about. I didn't give up, and neither did Mandi, and neither did Parker. Finally, a medicine that had been in Canada for quite some time had been approved by the FDA, and our doctor suggested we give it a shot. She has only had a few seizures since we started her on it. She used to have them nearly every night. That's commitment. Never give up. Surrender it to God, but never give up. If we're looking for a way out, we were never committed to begin with.

Mandi and I are commited to our little girl. We're devoted to our little boy. We're devoted to sharing God's love with folks and making our place survive. More than all of that, we're committed to God and each other. We've always said divorce is not an option. Murder is, but not divorce! That's what commitment is. There have been times that we've been so mad at each other we want to murder one another. Times I've screamed at her (without her being there) all the way to town for things she's done that I've asked her not to do, but we won't quit. We promised that.

God requires commitment from us, and Jesus is the perfect example of that. He committed to the cross, and he asks us to do the same. 2 Timothy 4:7 is what we should all want to be able to say when we meet God face to face: "I have fought the good fight, I have finished the race, I have kept the faith." That's commitment.

Paul's Miracles

Paul Davis was my animal science instructor back in my college days. I will say without qualification that Paul was *the* most enthusiastic teacher I have ever had in my life. That statement comes from a guy who spent more than his fair share sitting in the desks of higher institutions.

Whether he was teaching about how to figure out rations or about the reproductive cycle of a cow, Paul preached with the fire of a zealot. The notes he wrote on those white boards just drove the point home with passion. His back and forth between the class members was akin to a game being played. And everyone was the winner.

His greeting, "Okay, sports fans..." followed by whatever lesson he had planned set his tone like a Paul Harvey greeting. He'd ask for an answer from the audience, and when the correct answer came back his way, he'd respond, "Now, we're cooking with gas." Then he'd wink and click like he was trying to get his horse into the next gait.

We'd be in animal nutrition lab, and he'd provide us with several feedstuffs. Beautiful, green alfalfa hay that's measuring x in protein and y in TDN. He'd throw some corn silage in there. Then he'd turn us loose with some algebra and maybe a Pearson square. When we'd go over the problem, his marker would begin to fly. He'd take this, divide it by that, and, "Quick as cat! You've got a ration of z pounds of alfalfa and p pounds of corn per head per day until you run out!"

I'd love to listen to Paul tell us about the stages of gestation in a cow. He'd describe a calf at each stage, and his descriptions ranged from, "A tiny field mouse," to "A rat laying out on the beach at Waikiki." His enthusiasm and his color would keep our attention, and it would capture our passion, as well.

I think my passion for ruminant digestion came from Paul. My excitement about the reproductive cycle of cattle traces back to him and his smiling wink, as well. It was in Paul's classes where I was able to truly witness birth as a natural process, from the point of fertilization to the point of parturition. Each stage held something magnificent, whether it was a zygote traveling down the tube into the horn, an embryo attaching to the placenta, the placenta attaching to the uterine wall, or the calf exiting through the birth canal, the process truly amazed me.

Since those days of taking notes and preg checking for extra credit, I have taught students of my own the reproductive cycle, and I have always noted how *un*-accidental it truly is. It's amazing, and it happens perfectly nearly every time. I've heard so many people refer to it as *The Miracle of Birth*. Truthfully, though, it's not a miracle. An act of a mighty and gracious Creator, yes. A miracle, no. The process happens completely according to the natural laws God set into order when he created us in the first place. If the reproductive cycle is a miracle, then so is the earth spinning on its axis, a lung pulling in air with the help of a diaphragm, or a rock breaking off from a boulder and tumbling toward the earth with the help of a force called gravity.

Maybe that's it. Maybe everything God does just happens to be a miracle, and to me that's amazing. That's a God in whom I can trust. He obeys his own rules nearly all of the time. Jesus rising from the grave? That's a miracle. Everything else? God working the way he always does— in a way we can trust with every ounce of our being.

Francis Collins, a world-renowned scientist who believes in Jesus with all of his heart, worries that we may attribute the word *miracle* too haphazardly. I kind of agree. I want to say it's truly a miracle that 100 trillion cells in one body all have a strand of DNA, six feet long with three billion nucleotide pairs arranged in *perfect* order is a miracle. But it's not. That's the way God works. Your body just created who knows how many millions of those in an instant. That's how God works. He is just that awesome *all the time*! And we can trust him because he shows that he is faithful in all of the awesome things he does.

The miracle, in my opinion, is that he loves us enough to do so. The miracle is that he can change a heart. He can show his awesomeness by changing a hateful, angry, spiteful, and betraying heart into one of love, joy, peace and faithfulness simply by filling a person with his Spirit. That's a miracle. That's the fruit of the Spirit living within us. It's not magic. It's not some emotional high or crazy feeling. It's real. It's tangible. It's a miracle of God.

God is enough. The same God who makes the grass turn green every spring is just as faithful to give us a life of love, joy, peace, patience, kindness, goodness, faithfulness, gentleness, and self-control (Galatians 5:22-23) if we give him all we are. That's the miracle. And it's all that really matters, isn't it?

Practice, Practice, Practice

I made the mistake of telling my little boy a story I had heard about Roy Cooper. The fact that the story even registers with him is funny, as the Super Looper is a few years out of most eight-year-olds' frames of reference. But Crae, even though he's never seen the patriarch of the trio of current Cooper champions rope, is well aware that there must have been something great about a guy who could win eight gold buckles.

So when I told Crae a story that I had heard about Roy Cooper tying calves until his hands bled and then taping them up and tying them some more, Crae took it to heart. He got a goat tying dummy for his birthday, last summer, but for the most part it has sat in the corner of the living room gathering dust. Every now and then, he has gotten it out and tied it a few times, but he's never really practiced by any means.

However, buoyed by some pretty nice awards he received for his top four finishes in all of his events last year at the junior rodeos, Crae decided it was time to get to work. He asked me, "Dad, how many times did that guy tie calves until his hands bled?" I told him a hundred, just hoping he'd tie his dummy twenty times or so. The little booger grabbed a pen and paper and started tying. He'd tally each run or have me do it, and by about run number twenty, he had it down pretty well.

At about run number thirty-five, his finger started getting a little tender from pulling his hooey through so well. It was pretty cool to watch. In thirty-five runs, he had gone from having to get told how to do it all over again to making really smooth runs that were picking up more and more speed and aggression with each flank of the dummy. Of course, Mandi, who was a pretty studly goat tyer in her day, was on hand to point out some of the finer points of keeping a goat tied, studying the boys ahead of him, and looking the goats over before the rodeo. It was fun to see Crae just lighting up with every success.

He looked at me and said, "Man, this is fun. I'm getting better."

I told him, "Yep. Pretty quick, it will be automatic."

"You think Gator Goodrich has one of these dummies?" he asked.

I told him I thought Gator probably had every gadget in the book. I told him, "For Pete's sake, his dad's been to the NFR a bunch in the calf roping, so I'm sure he's got everything it takes to get really good, if he wants to work at it."

Crae said, "Well, practice is what it takes to get good," and he flanked that goat again.

By the time Crae had gotten to sixty, he had made several flawless runs, and it was becoming automatic. He had tape on a couple of fingers. I told him he needed to quit. He argued, "But I've only got forty to go, and I'm not bleeding yet." We told him he needed to be able to do it again tomorrow, and he agreed. "One more perfect one, though." He stuck it on one more and put the tied goat back in the corner.

He and I were talking about it after he finished, and he told me he wanted to be one of the big boys. I said, "You know what it takes?"

He told me, "It all comes down to three words, Dad: practice, practice, practice."

I laughed. "Yeah, and rich parents."

I don't know if Crae will ever be one of the big boys in any of his events. But I *am* glad he's finally figuring out that it takes work to be good at something. We were talking about a show we had watched during the Olympics about raising Olympians. Mikaela Shiffrin's parents had instilled in her that the fun in any sport was being good because of all of the work one had put into it. Because of that, Mikaela has a passion for drills, for working out, for all of the monotonous exercises that allow her to be the best in the world at skiing a slalom course. Crae's been paying attention to that a little more all the time. The person who works the hardest usually ends up winning.

I remember my favorite *No Fear* t-shirt from twenty years ago. Emblazoned across the piece of clothing were the words, "Someone, somewhere is practicing right now, and when you meet him in head to head competition, he'll beat you." That's the truth in athletics, with very few exceptions.

I suppose it's pretty true in life, as well. If we're not moving forward, we're moving backward. If we're not seeking life, we're settling for death. If we're not disciplined enough to keep walking toward God, we're slack enough to fall away from him.

Hebrews 12:11 says, "No discipline seems pleasant at the time, but painful. Later on, however, it produces a harvest of righteousness and peace for those who have been trained by it." Sometimes, it's pretty hard to make the right choice, the one that leads us to the life Jesus offers. But it's critical to making it across the finish line in the race that Paul tells us we should run to win.

The Mulberry Leaf

When I had big aspirations of being a saddle maker, I used to go and hang out with some of the guys who did it right. My hope was that their skills would rub off on me and that I would in turn become one of the greats. One of those guys I used to go visit quite a little bit was Rich Boyer.

Visiting with Rich was always fun. He had lived life as a cowboy for a lot of years and had naturally progressed into becoming a craftsman who had built some of the best saddles a guy could hope to ride. I had gotten to know Rich through my rodeo years, and when I decided to study the saddle making craft, I thought he'd be the guy.

Different from many saddle makers, Rich was pretty adept at continuing his work while visiting. He'd carry on while telling stories, asking me what I'd been up to, and describing his process. About the only time he'd stop working is if he had a joke to tell. He'd stand up straight, blink a couple of times and begin telling the joke. Rich would get such a kick out of it that laughing at him was almost as natural as laughing at his tale.

Rich's style of tooling was pretty unique. He had a diamond pattern that he'd put on a lot of his saddles in lieu of any of several types of typical stamps. His tooling was bold, and his flowers unique. His diamond A brand was always prominent on his maker's mark, and the ride in those saddles was worth every penny a guy had to pay for one of them.

One of his patterns, unique to Rich, was that of a mulberry leaf. He told me that one day he found a leaf floating down the irrigation ditch behind his house. Watching it float downstream, Rich noticed it would be quite the addition to a piece of his leather art. He pulled it from the water and took it back to draw it up as a pattern. He carved it on a piece of leather or two before he decided to take the plant to the extension office to see what it was.

The extension agent told Rich that it was a mulberry leaf, and that pleased him. He looked at me and said, "You know, I was a little worried that I might be tooling a marijuana leaf on my saddles." I agreed that might be bad for business.

Rich would work day in and day out in his shop in the upstairs of Roemark's western store in Hermiston. He'd take a day off once in a while to go ride with friends after cows, but most days he kept his nose to the grindstone. He made saddles for the Pendleton Round Up, the Farm-City Prorodeo, the Columbia River Circuit, and the PRCA's Announcer of the Year. The thing I like most about Rich's saddles is that a guy could go rope steers in one just as easily and readily as go cowboy all day in one. They are just good, all-around saddles.

Although he's slowed his saddlemaking down to building them for family, Rich is still known as a top tier craftsman. I think his reputation can be attributed to saddles that turned out so good because of his consistent work ethic. He never looked up from the job except to tell a joke or two. That was his way of enjoying the company that had dropped by to visit.

That's a good pattern by which we can live our lives. Keep our heads down and working, but come up to enjoy those around us once in a while. Then get back to work. There's joy in work, and there's joy in a job well done. Rich is a great example of that.

In Genesis, we see where God made Adam and put him in the garden to work. He was to take dominion, to do good things with his hands, and that was before the curse. Work was good. In Chapter 2:15, it says, "The Lord God took the man and put him in the Garden of Eden to work it and take care of it." That's a big part of our purpose. We are also blessed with people to love, and that's important, too. Rich's habits point to the fruits both of work and of enjoying those around you. He turned out saddles people loved, and he's got friends who'd lay their lives down for him. He wins on both accounts.

The Steens

The beautiful Steens Mountain rises up gradually from the tiny hamlet of Frenchglen, Oregon not too far from the cattle baron, Pete French's, P Ranch. Littered with sage, juniper and aspens, the mountain's snow covered silhouette can be seen from a hundred miles away, if you're in the right part of the country. Once you have reached the top, you can look down the beautiful Kiger Gorge, or ride your pony out and have lunch overlooking the Little Blitzen Gorge. The coolest sight on the Steens Mountain is when you're standing on the edge of it, looking almost straight down to the Alvord Desert. It truly drops straight off on the Southeast side, and it's awesome.

On that Alvord Desert below is the historic Alvord Ranch on which Bob Campbell buckarooed in the years prior to World War II. Bob Campbell was my grandpa, and it was a great joy to hear his stories over the years about the way things changed across time. Today, the Steens Mountain is a national monument, signed out of use by Bill Clinton in his feverish lame duck blockading of multiple use in the arid west. Back then, it was a grazier's paradise, and it was used by a number of ranchers in that neck of the woods. My wife and I rode up there and rode through a couple of sheepherders and their flocks, but there wasn't a cow track to be seen. But in the days of common sense and true management--natural management--it put pounds on thousands of head of beef.

It would be summer before cattle would run on the Steens, at least up in the high parts. The snow stays until the end of May and into June, but by the time the cattle arrived, the grass was green, and it was tall. Grandpa said the cattle ate it down pretty good, and when the time came for the cattle to go home (which they usually started doing on their own), the grass was pretty well eaten off. No matter, the last guy off the mountain would light it on fire. That fire would take everything with it that wasn't wet. It managed the juniper. It kept the sagebrush and rabbit brush from taking over, and when God started it all to grow in the spring, it was a completely new creation, ready for another year of grazing.

That's about what God does to us when we accept Jesus' gift of a rescued life of freedom--when we make him Lord of our lives. I'm not talking about the burning down part; I'm talking about the new life part. Everything that had been torn up and burned down by sin and trying to do it our own way became a completely new creation when we gave our hearts to the only one who can truly heal them. 2 Corinthians 5:17 says, "Therefore, if anyone is in Christ, he is a new creation; the old had gone, the new has come!" We don't have to change any more than an overgrazed section of pasture had to change. We can't clean our acts up, and we don't need to. When we accept Jesus, he does it. He gives us new life--completely new life. And if you haven't done that yet, you're missing out on the real deal. Invite him in. The grass really is greener on that side.

Flattery Stinks

Bucking horse names can be some of the coolest monikers a person will hear. I have always enjoyed the ones who are named after colorful characters of the West: Jackson Sundown, Will James, Calamity Jane, Charlie Russell, Chief Joseph, Wicked Felina and even Khadafy. Khadafy is actually *way* West of the Pecos, but it's still a colorful handle. Nevertheless, I always thought that if a guy was cool enough to get a bucking horse tagged after him, he must be all right. That idea flew out the window when Andy Ely named a bucking horse for me.

The story behind the name is the worst part.

We were practicing out at Andy's place in Juniper Canyon one afternoon, and I had had the flu all night long and into the day. I had stayed home from school to heal up, and it hadn't worked. I was still pretty sick, both the top and bottom ends of me. As we were standing around waiting, I was pretty quiet. Rowdy Barry happened to notice, and he interrogated me a bit. I told him I probably should have stayed home instead of coming to get on. I wasn't sure how far away from the outhouse I was going to get. He said, "Well, don't get on. If you're sick, that's as good a reason as any."

Jokingly, I told him, "That's all right, Rowdy. I brought an extra pair of undershorts in my bag."

Before long, I was putting my saddle on a little brown horse that was about as hard as a rock. The muscle-bound pony had only been bucked a time or two, and they weren't real sure what his trip was. About ready to throw up, I poured myself into the bucking chute and, quivering like a leaf, I put on my stirrups. I nodded my head.

The first jump was stellar. I marked that dude out, and he did fire. He cracked 'em about four jumps straight out from the chute, and he was strong! I guess things were looking pretty good from the outside, but inside, I was just hoping to survive. The fifth jump, that little horse bogged his head and sucked back, sending me right over the dashboard. My left foot stayed in the stirrup and whipped me down underneath of him where his back two feet stepped right in the middle of me when he jumped for the sixth time. When he kicked, his front foot came right down the side of my face. The only thing anyone could see that looked hopeful was the fact that my stirrup came off my foot.

Sick, in pain, and in La La Land, I curled up in the fetal position with my head resting in the dirt. Pat Beard, who was picking up, rode over, got off his horse, and kneeled down beside me. Rowdy had been pulling gates, and he was right there, as well. They both thought I was hurt. Pat asked me, "Are you okay?"

I groaned and answered, "I'm just glad I didn't mess my pants."

Pat started laughing hysterically, but Rowdy responded, "I thought you brought an extra pair of shorts." I shook my head and told him I had only been kidding. I got up, survived and watched Andy's horse, *Marty* run around the arena one more lap. The only saving grace for me was that the horse did buck hard. The judges would mark him high, but he had a tendency to buck so hard he'd cripple himself for a while. I figured that was worth something.

I guess I should have been flattered that Andy named *Marty* after me. But I wasn't. Instead of me giving into that temptation of being flattered, I always felt a little bit embarrassed about the horse's handle. Flattery can be tempting, but many times we need to realize that the story behind it is a bad case of the scours. Chief Joseph had horses named after him because he was a great leader. I got one named after me because I was able to refrain from being stuck with dirty trousers. Not a story to tell over and over, although it has been, and now, it's in writing.

I've been approached about jobs or positions where people sing my praises and make me feel really, really good about myself. Upon later inspection, though, I realize that the position will probably hurt me or distract me, and the enemy knows that. However, that flattery makes it hard to resist. I've learned, with God's help, that flattery usually has something more odiferous behind it. It should stink. Proverbs 29:5 says, "Whoever flatters his neighbor is spreading a net for his feet." That's about the truth. When somebody is blowing sunshine up our noses, we need to look at the situation with Jesus. He'll show us the good and bad. The enemy won't, and that's why flattery stinks.

GROUSE FLATS

Overlooking the Grande Ronde River near Troy, Oregon is a bench several miles up called Grouse Flats. To get there from Troy, one would take the old Bartlett Road and just keep driving up. In that beautiful expanse of rolling fields surrounded by pine trees are the remnants of an old post office. A rotten chunk of wood here, a rusty nail there. Perhaps even a piece of shattered glass litters the ground every so often. Whatever's left, however, is merely the dust from a house that raised my Grandpa Chuck Gooding.

From a young age, my grandpa grew up in the old log post office. His brother Frank owned the place, and being much older and the eldest living son of Archibald Gooding, Frank took his mother and siblings in after Archie passed away. Grandpa loved living around Troy, and the stories of all the places and people that I have heard over the years have always made me long to have a piece of that life to call my own.

That feeling was common to my whole family, and in 1997, my parents purchased the dilapidated post office, which had fallen most of the way in on itself. The purchase included the building and its surrounding outbuildings, and on an October day, several of us, including Grandma and Grandpa made the trek from my parents' house in Wallowa to Troy. Mandi and I had been dating for five months, and on that trip, she learned how crazy this family really was.

When we got up there, Grandpa was like a kid in a candy store. My aunt Tammi was video recording him as he told stories and stopped to remember each place and all of the sepia toned memories he found running through his mind. He had just had a heart attack, so we were under express orders to keep him from doing any heavy lifting. It didn't work. He bailed in, anyway. We loaded up all of the logs and boards we could, and we hauled them to my parents' place until we could figure out what to do with them.

Over the years, we all had different items made from that old post office in which my grandpa spent his childhood. What makes it the coolest is that my grandpa created nearly every item. He was a fine craftsman for decades, and his skills at turning old wood into art were truly amazing. For him to have been able to change that house of his into furniture for the rest of us is truly a blessing. For Mandi and me, our most prominently displayed piece of that history is the mantle on our fireplace. Grandpa took a couple of the last logs and turned them into a stunning mantle that not only holds memories on its topside, but holds memories in itself.

When Mandi and I got married, we started having Grandpa make all of our furniture. Our end tables, coffee table, entertainment center, picture frames, coat racks, a trunk and a corner cabinet all bear the signature of Chuck Gooding. Much of that was made from boards from Mandi's grandpa, Pat Trimble's, barn. My grandpa planed them and turned them into art that we still have today. To me, it's awesome to have so much of my family history surrounding me. Grandpa was born in 1920, and his last big carpentry project was turning his shop into an apartment for him and my grandma. That was when he was 90. He ramrodded that project and worked the days away until it was finished.

He and my grandma Charlotte spent a lot of summers, evenings, and weekends looking after my brother and me when we were little. They are both very special to us, and every day I look around my house to see furniture made out of wood that watched him grow up, it inspires me. It's like no matter where I go, there's a piece of them close by. I don't see them near as much as I'd like, but they're never really that far away.

That's like having God's Word buried in our hearts. As long as we have his Word, he's never very far away. As a matter of fact, the Holy Spirit actually lives in us. There's always a reminder of his love, his plan, and his desires for how we should live our lives. There's always a reminder of his miracles, his passions, and his grace. His Word is a constant reminder.

Prayer constantly links us to him, just like talking to and listening to our closest friend. In reality, it *is* communicating with our closest friend.

Psalm 119:10-11 says, "I seek you with all my heart; do not let me stray from your commands. I have hidden your Word in my heart that I might not sin against you." When God's Word is hidden in our hearts, life becomes good. Not necessarily easy or perfect, but good. That's plenty for me.

Marty Campbell, his wife, Mandi, and their children, Parker and Crae, minister to the cowboy world through Broken Horn Ranch Ministries, out of Pendleton, Oregon. They have a mission of bringing Jesus to the western world through western events and regular fellowship, introducing people to a real God who cares about their real lives.

Made in the USA
Lexington, KY
14 October 2015